A COUNTRYMAN'S DIARY

A COUNTRYMAN'S DIARY

The reflections of a village parson

*"Dedicated to my dearest wife, Angela,
who shared my love of the countryside and
who introduced me to Jack Russell terriers".*

by John Green

SALMON

Published by J. Salmon Limited
100 London Road, Sevenoaks, Kent TN13 1BB

First Edition 2000

Designed by the Salmon Studio

Text copyright © John Green
Illustrations copyright © 2000 J. Salmon Limited

ISBN 1-902842-12-X

Printed in England
by J. Salmon Limited
Tubs Hill Works, Sevenoaks.

Illustrations

Line drawings

Photographs

Foreword

The publication of this my third book on country life naturally gives me great pleasure. Those of you who have read my earlier books and who also perhaps read me week by week in the local paper, will know enough about the background of my writings. However, it is possible that this book may attract some completely new readers from near or far away, so I must obey my publishers' request for a Foreword. Of necessity, though, it includes background material that will be familiar to some, and I hope they will forgive me or move on immediately to Chapter One.

I suppose that my love of the countryside all began in a Kent cherry orchard. My father's spacious rectory was surrounded on three sides by cherry orchards and beyond them were acres of hop gardens. My daily walks became a joy and an education. Small boys are naturally inquisitive so questions flowed and knowledge unconsciously grew. Specially exciting was cherry-picking time; cherries seemed to shower down onto the ground and we daily returned with a basket overflowing. Then came hop-picking in September, with the invasion of East Enders from London and its own special camaraderie in the hop gardens. Later, my father moved across the County and his new country parish embraced a large heronry and some of Romney Marsh. New discoveries, new bird life and the romantic atmosphere of the Marsh and, unknowingly I was captivated and fell in love with that Fifth Quarter of the Globe.

Then in the background were my two uncles - one a botanist and the other a well-known entomologist, his large study full of boxes and apparatus and cabinets. Open them and you might see a privet hawk moth caterpillar or rows of fritillaries. It was not long before he enthused me and gave me a sound and sensitive understanding of that fascinating and gentle world of moth and butterfly. Years later, I had the privilege of my own country parishes in Kent. Large rectory gardens were surrounded by the whole range of countryside - open marshland, downland (with orchids), cherry orchards and hop gardens and the undulating Wealden farmland. Regularly involved in writing sermons and letters and articles for my parish magazine, I soon felt impelled to write about the countryside as well and to open people's eyes to the wonders around them daily. So "A Countryman's Notebook" was born and introduced into the magazine and the local paper.

Some twenty years later, retirement from my two lovely Wealden parishes of Sandhurst and Newenden came about. Just before this happened, appreciative friends and parishioners persuaded me to put together a collection of these articles under the title of "From a Country Rectory Window". This seemed an obvious title. All my articles had been written at my study desk beside a window. From my chair I had enjoyed a view of my large garden and, across the valley, of my parish church of St. Nicholas, set on a hill which dipped steeply down to the Kent Ditch and the River Rother. Endless inspiration came from that view. Strawberry pickers in the next field, chaffinches nesting in the hedge, pheasants strolling through the paddock, autumn colouring of Norway maples - all this and more lay before my eyes through the year. Hence the origin of the first of my three books on country life.

I hope that you enjoy this third collection, illustrated most sympathetically by my friend, Stephen Message. Although it is arranged to span a year, it is not strictly the writings of one year only, so occasionally there is more than one reference to the same annual event of a particular month.

There is also reference to two Jack Russells, Oliver and Brock; they were in turn our stimulating canine companions over the years from which these entries were chosen. Oliver, who was supreme among our succession of Jack Russells, was tragically run over outside our house. For the sake of authenticity and affection, I have purposely kept to the original names. All our Jack Russells have been our friends and our family. I also need to thank one or two people. This book is dedicated to my wife, Angela, which is a special honour, intended to underline her enormous influence in this and in every part of my life. In addition, I owe a great deal to Mr. John Piper and the Wealden Advertiser for giving me an outlet for many years and for their friendliness and cooperation. Thirdly, I owe a lot to my publishers, J. Salmon Ltd., who have always given me much encouragement and advice ever since Mr. Derek Salmon and I enthused each other into producing my first quite attractive little book.

I still long to be a tiny cog in the ever-growing movement to understand and care for our countryside and its wildlife, under constant threat from the demands of our modern, technological society. This threat is particularly strong at present in my beloved Kent, once fondly named the Garden of England. I also long to help people tune in to the balance and slow rhythm of the countryside, so that, in the end, every walk is full of interest, every day seems a holiday and in every direction they can see God.

Rolvenden, Kent 1999   John Green

JANUARY

We all live on hope. Christmas is the greatest hope but, at the other end of the scale, most of us live in the hope of another day. Within that concept, many tiny things liven us up during the day. Yesterday, December 29, I suddenly realised, at 4 pm after a dullish day, that I could see the length of my field and at 400 yards still distinguish shades of colour in the hedge. This would not have been possible a week ago. Hope! The days were already a fraction longer, by about seven minutes. To stay in that mood a little longer, I opened Charles Tunnicliffe's lovely "Shorelands Winter Diary" and turned to Christmas Day. It was sunrise and, to his joy, he heard and saw and later painted a 30 strong flight of white-fronted geese as they flew low over the dark chimneys of the cottages. Beside this evocative painting he wrote "From now on, the sun in his rising will be moving a little more to the eastward and when he appears behind Snowdon's peak we shall know that the winter has not much longer to reign". Words of hope.

Most gardens show signs of hope even now. In my own case, the daffodils are fore-most in reminding us of Spring, but no sign of my snowdrops, which may have been casualties of vigorous winter tidying. The primulas are bravely showing a touch of colour and hoping for a few mild days in January in which to offer a cluster of reds, yellows and blues. Both my lilacs are showing lots of leaf bud, but my special delight is in my small pink camellia near the road; it bears 20 or more buds, more than ever before. Could it be due to all those tea-leaves I laboriously gave it in the autumn? I do so hope that many readers watched "A Winter's Tale" on BBC2 on Boxing Day. It was a real masterpiece of photography and of study of wildlife in the Winter. A delight to the eye of the countryman, even though its vividness made one feel cold and windswept. One could not help but marvel at the resilience of quite small waders, heads tucked into plumage and crowded together on some gale-swept coast. Whooper swans (from Greenland), white-fronted geese, barn owls, foxes, water-voles (with young), a sleeping dormouse, all passed before us, with the briefest of commentary, thank goodness. After raging storms, we found ourselves in the utter silence and semi-darkness of a ruined tower, the winter shelter for numerous bats and peacock butterflies. Full marks to the BBC Natural History Unit. A Happy New Year to you all!

"God speed the plough!" - prayerful words spoken yesterday in All Saints, Staplehurst. The old-fashioned plough had been carried up the aisle to the sanctuary by local farmers, led by the two churchwardens. A survival from pre-Reformation times, when Plough Monday was the first resumption of work after the great Christmas feast; yet not much work was done, more likely processions and jollification and lighting of plough candles. Maybe, though, it is a helpful survival. It takes our thoughts away from computers and television to basic things. As one historian puts it:

> "The plough remains the symbol of civilisation, for it enables man to cease
> his nomadic life and become a settler and a builder ... it was the instrument
> by which he fulfilled the divine command to subdue the earth..."

Moreover, ever since, most farmers have known in their heart of hearts that they have an unwritten partnership with the Almighty. So - "God speed the plough! that the people of our land may be satisfied with bread".

Bread is hopefully going to result from the winter wheat in the fields on the Rother Levels near me. It is hard work, though, for the wheat - little warmth and still quite a few hungry rabbits. Our Jack Russell, Oliver, does his very best to keep them on the move and occasionally catches them. Sometimes amusing things happen. Last week he was chasing one along the dyke when it suddenly saw me and turned about, only to run head-on into Oliver, who in turn did a somersault and pursued it with strangled yelps. Or again, the week before, Oliver was on a hot scent, parallel to me, among the reeds and willows, when there was a scrabbling noise about my head and a Jack Russell muzzle appeared out of a hollow willow trunk. Question - where was the rabbit being pursued?!

Nature invariably poses questions. A knowledgeable friend was recently puzzled by numerous empty shells of the swan mussel, usually lying on top of the banks of the dykes or river. Although near the water's edge, there were no discernible footprints at all. Who had taken them - mink, heron or human? Almost certainly gulls, according to another expert friend; they carry them aloft, extract and eat and then drop the shells. The countryside generally remains rather "grey", but some gardens are offering us a bit of cheer. Besides the jasmine and the daphne, the winter-flowering prunus "autumnalis" is in numerous places giving us a foretaste of Spring blossom, with its

delicate pinky-white flowers. But special cheer came yesterday from the centre of a wallflower plant - a hibernating ladybird was testing the air.

At last, two Spring-like days in succession. Wonderfully uplifting, after days of rain and mud. My rain gauge recorded 66.5 mm in December. Surprise at such a low total was explained by the fact that rain fell on 15 days out of the 31 in the month, thereby giving the impression of unending rain. To show how fortunate we have been, the weatherman on the 9 o'clock News last night, Twelfth Night, nonchalantly announced that 65 mm of rain had fallen that day in the north-west "and more flooding was expected".

In spite of the comparatively low rainfall, most ponds are full and very muddy. Fields along the Hexden Channel route have some standing water, notably near the old mill at Eaglesden, but lacking the usual gulls and lapwings. Potman's Heath Channel was almost as wide as the length of a cricket pitch on the 5th. Half a mile north, a small plantation of cricket bat willows were mostly standing in water; they will not mind, of course, though winter wheat does suffer from more than a week of those conditions.Last night I rather sadly took down my Christmas cards. When they first pour in through the letter-box, they may initially cause alarm as well as pleasure, pleasure that old friends have not forgotten us and sent news, but alarm that we may have forgotten them. Nevertheless, for a fortnight or so, they have transformed our mantle-pieces, stairs, desks and cupboards. They have daily given us a colourful, pictorial and perhaps religious message - of friendship and faith. We all need those two factors to carry us through life.

Today, as I write, is the Feast of the Epiphany. The original Greek word gives us the theme "manifestation", but often overshadowed by that of "offering". The spectacle of the Magi worshipping the Child in the manger has always been an inspiration to both Eastern and Western Churches - the contrasts of simplicity and splendour, the mystery of those offerings. My Oxford Dictionary of the Christian Church tells me -

"In England the sovereign makes offerings of gold, frankincense
and myrrh in the Chapel Royal on the feast."

So I look in the Court Circular of my paper. I see no hint of our Queen's movements. Security, of course, but ironic and sad. Christ came to bring peace.

Yesterday a wood-pigeon flew across my line of vision, as I looked out of my window. It landed in the lilac near the gate and stayed there, so I watched it. I soon realised, to my fury, that it was enjoying the tender leaf-buds. No wonder that the entry against its name in the Reader's Digest "Book of British Birds" begins - "No bird is a greater enemy of the British farmer than the gentle-looking wood-pigeon... practically all the year round, it ravages crops... clover, sainfoin, newly sown grain in the early January-March period..". Another writer, R. C. Robertson-Glasgow in his "Country Talk" rails against poetic favouritism and declares "This bird is nothing more than a tough and impudent rascal, and can have nothing whatever to moan about except, possibly, indigestion arising from gross gluttony". My wood-pigeon remained in situ for 20 minutes, only to flap a yard or so onto the macricarpa hedge, selecting seeds and green shoots for another 20 minutes. The farmer's remedy of the "banger" would drive Brock into the furthest corner of the house.

Fortunately, I have other more acceptable birds on the other side, facing south-west. There has been the traditional January spectacle in my field of mixed flocks of field-fares, redwings, lapwings and the occasional rook from Frensham rookery. They descend periodically and quietly during a day, forage for half an hour and then try another likely field, before paying a return date later. My garden birds are fairly representative but do not include greenfinches or enough tits - where, are those small bands of long-tailed tits that frequent old orchards and spill over into nearby gardens when food is scarce? It is always worth studying the "foraging habits" of your birds. The bird-table may be central to your feeding but it can be dominated by the bully-boys - starlings, collared-doves and rooks - for the first half hour, so I always spread my seed, crumbs and apple peelings in other quieter, shrub areas where my blackbirds, chaffinches and robin explore daily.

The other day I was having coffee and chat in a house with a large garden and numerous rhododendrons. I had always regarded it as a paradise for any Jack Russell - rabbits abounded. That morning I watched two foxes conducting a known military tactic - a pincer movement on a large rhododendron. We never knew the result. A local fox demonstrated typical sangfroid the same week. Notwithstanding that the hunt had moved off from Great Maytham hardly an hour before, he trotted slowly along the southern terrace before doing the same patrol at the front, which must have been almost vibrant with the smell of dogs and people. Full marks to "Charlie" for boldness. I love to see him, but I do not, of course, keep chickens.

Twelfth Night is long past and most of us are already alert for signs of Spring. In our small garden one of the first heralds of better things is our lilac which has had green buds since before Christmas. Daffodils and crocus are, of course, well above ground but this week two clumps of snowdrops came into flower, as did also some wild primroses under a sheltering bush. These tiny portents are encouraging in view of these lines from an early "Calendar of English Flowers" -

> "The snowdrop in purest white arraie,
> First rears her hedde on Candlemas day;
> While the crocus hastens to the shrine
> Of Primrose love on St. Valentine."

There is no sign yet of my iris reticulata whose scented violet blue flowers were showing well last January, according to my diary. However, a friend's garden in Hawkhurst can improve on my own and boasts of aconites in flower for a week and a pink camellia (not normally early) bearing half a dozen blooms. Further afield, walking the dog, I see oak buds showing red brown but the majority of catkins are still very stubby, another contrast to my diary entry for 13 January 1994 "saw lengthening hazel catkins all around me". It may have been possible this week to garden up to 4.30 pm but the wise gardener is probably spending more time in his greenhouse, watching over his sweet pea seeds and geraniums and cacti.

Bewl Water seems fuller than I can remember of recent years but I am told that the water is three feet lower than the high mark on its banks. It is always good for body and mind to stop there at any point and walk and observe. Wind and rain had driven dog walkers and nature-lovers away yesterday and only a few Canadas and grey-lag geese were afloat, with a little grebe ploughing a lonely furrow near the shore. One or two cormorants are, I believe, present, probably to the fury of the fishermen; readers may know that their increasing numbers in some areas has led to a licence for shooting in South Wales. Unexpectedly present over Christmas at the end of Wards Lane was a blackpoll warbler, usually resident half in Canada and half in South America. Twitchers were numerous enough to merit a special car-park. Readers may also not know that Bewl Water is 20 years old this year and this period has allowed the expert landscaping time enough to mature. At least one resident on the Water spoke how lovely the shores look this winter, it being difficult now to differentiate between the natural trees and the planting. Much credit to Dame Elizabeth Crowe, the architect.

Next Sunday brings an unknown Saint's day, with a connection with the countryside, St. Vincent. A Spanish martyr, he died after torture on the orders of Diocletian and is in some places the patron of wine growers. Hence the rhyme -

> "If on St. Vincent day the sky is clear,
> More wine than water will crown the year"

My study on the first floor enjoys a pleasing rural view. From my desk I look across fields to the Rother Valley and the Northiam ridge beyond. But in the immediate foreground is a seven acre field bordering our garden and today at 12 noon it presents a typical mid-January scene. About 70 ewes in lamb are distributed evenly all over the field, the majority lying down, having had a breakfast of rolled oats from the troughs in the middle and finishing it off with mouthfuls of hay from the rack in the corner, sheltered a little from the worst of the weather. The troughs are now turned over and a few latecomers are having brunch at the hay-rack. But the field is alive with movement, even if most of the ewes are lying down. Among the sheep are 50 or more gulls, some circling lazily overhead and others strolling languidly around, occasionally digging out a worm. In addition, there are at least two dozen rooks interspersed among sheep and gulls. A few are scavenging round the troughs for remainders, others are competing for the earthworms, one is on the back of a sheep investigating its wool, and six are perched along our fence like funeral bearers waiting for the service to begin and for their lunch afterwards. A few swash-buckling starlings and one magpie complete the picture. Every few minutes there occurs a mysterious alarm and the whole lot rise in semi-panic, circle and then re-distribute themselves over the field. The sheep, of course, remain unmoved and continue chewing placidly.

Such a picture must be repeated endlessly in sheep-rearing countryside. Whilst it may not be exciting to many onlookers, it is to me stabilising and reassuring of the slow rhythm and fertility of the countryside. A similar feeling came to me later that day as I paused at the lambing sheds at Hoads Farm, Sandhurst. Four hundred ewes were in pens on deep straw, watched over by David, the shepherd, and his dogs. Twelve lambs had already arrived and were being prepared for the open field, the beginnings of a great inflow of new life on that farm from 850 ewes in all. Such has been the rainfall though (2 inches in the past week in my gauge) that many fields are more waterlogged than they have been for years and the weight of the ewes in our field has inevitably resulted in its being heavily pockmarked from one boundary fence to the other, poor conditions for both feet and grass.

I was so very pleased to read in my "Times" today that Sir David Attenborough had yesterday presented an action plan, entitled "Biodiversity Challenge" to John Gummer to save 600 British species of flora and fauna. Among the birds listed are the song thrush and the skylark, both species which many of us country-dwellers grew up to take for granted, as well as the high-profile bittern; the latter, normally resident in the reed beds of Norfolk and Suffolk, are now down to an incredible 16 pairs. To me a dreadful reflection on our society and its attitudes. I suspect that the brown hare may also be in David Attenborough's list. Intensive agriculture seems to have decimated the numbers of this exciting and noble creature. When we lived in Romney Marsh 30 years ago, hares were a daily sight. I believe they are still to be seen in counties like Norfolk, Cambridgeshire and Buckinghamshire but not in Kent. It is just possible that the controversial set aside scheme may be a limited lifeline for this lovely animal.

FEBRUARY

The 9 o'clock News is imminent and I have my feet in front of a roaring log fire and a Jack Russell stretched out beside me. With the temperature outside below freezing and frost gradually whitening my car and lawn, I can ask nothing better than one's own hearth and fireside.

Wildlife has had, of course, to adapt to this recent spell of cold and frost by night and to a lesser extent by day. Birds and mammals come closer to humans. Birdtables are more patronised and sightings of badgers and foxes more frequent. On my early dog walk today I saw new little diggings by a badger or badgers at regular intervals along a grass verge by an overgrown copse. Their noses must have indicated a good chance of finding worms or grubs along this stretch, and they investigated quite methodically. Several friends have had foxes recently in their gardens, particularly round birdtables on which are placed fatty scraps. In the prevailing conditions birds can be very regular, almost demanding. One Hawkhurst friend, besides the usual garden species, has a song thrush call every day for a feed of currants and three cock and two hen pheasants expect food every morning and evening. In my own case, I suppose, my most regular and punctual are three or four blackbirds and two collared-doves, who are always perched, expectant, on the fence or tree by 8 am.

In this Weald and Rother countryside there has recently been a noticeable increase in lapwings and fieldfares. For a week I have watched 50 or more fieldfares spending all day, foraging and enjoying the sun in the field behind me. Reports of large lapwing flocks have come from places as far apart as Staplehurst, the Rother Valley and Camber; in the latter case, about 2,000, with golden plovers among them. Good news, after reports last year of declining numbers.

The lapwing happens to be also the logo for the Wiltshire Wildlife Trust and by chance I was in Wiltshire yesterday, Candlemas or the Presentation of Christ in the

Temple. The occasion was the funeral of a cousin, a distinguished soldier and County Councillor, and the country church was packed. It was made more moving by the presence of a bugler from the Royal Artillery, in dress uniform and headgear, who sounded the Last Post and the Reveille, as we prepared to process out. Later, on reflection, I realised that those bugle calls were in tune with the Feast Day and that equally moving occasion in the temple, 2,000 years ago, and old Simeon's words. They might be summarised -

"Lord, I can die happy now...a light has been born that will never go out".

I write further on Candlemas Day. Beside being a festival of the Church, it has also inspired numerous customs and traditions, especially in the country. After attending church for candles to be blessed, lighted and distributed, parishioners used to process with them round church and village. The motive was, I fear, more superstitious than religious - to guard against evil spirits and storms. The day has also inspired many old sayings. The one I rather prefer is -

"When Candlemas is come and gone
The snow lieth on a hot stone".

It is a comforting thought. We are now into February and now, if it comes, snow is unlikely to stay long.

The photographer and the artist, as well as children, may revel in the snow but it also offers an exciting opportunity to the naturalist - tracks of wildlife are visible, and tracks often lead to tunnels. Sometimes these are simply holes in thick hedges or at the bottom of a wire fence. Sometimes they are longish tunnels through a mass of grass and reeds, as alongside the old drovers' track where Oliver and I often walk. Local rabbits have made them day by day and Oliver dives into them at speed in pursuit. In a way these tracks and tunnels are like wildlife footpaths — the shortest route from home to food or water or friends, exactly as the original country footpaths, now rather official and signposted. In a stretch of only 150 yards of wire fencing on a local farm, I spotted three well-used holes and yet I knew that the nearest rabbits were at least 200 yards away; so could they have been made by foxes, who travel further than rabbits anyway? Forensic experts might find some tiny pieces of fur on the wire. They certainly would on a hole under the wire surrounding Rolvenden Layne play area; I am fairly sure that it is used by a fox patrolling between Frensham and Lowden Farm.

In general the countryside is full of encouraging hints and suggestions of Spring. Early camellia buds are showing streaks of pink, some japonicas (often on house walls) have a few red flowers, iris reticulata are adding their rich purple and yellow, and the first lambs have arrived in the lambing shed on Hoads Farm, Sandhurst. Not

so in Romney Marsh, however. Most farmers wait, often until their traditional date, 1st of April. Some diversify these days and grow oil seed rape, as well as cereals. An increasing problem for these crops in that area is swans. A recent news item reported a flock of 200 bewick swans moving from field to field. My friend, Gordon, a keen naturalist as well as farmer, talked darkly about the need to cull. These birds will need more than the usual "bangers" to scare them away.

Most of you will know that St. Valentine's Day approaches. Local shops remind you of it and adapt all sorts of goods to fit the theme. Local hostelleries play their part by offering 6-course gourmet dinners, with appropriate but mysterious titles to dishes, like "lover's sauce" on pork. One pub, the Man of Kent, excelled itself over its menu descriptions; each course and each dish within the course bore tantalising headings, such as "Seductive Steak" and "It had to be Ewe". They deserve to be fully booked. All this is rather a far cry from the traditional favourite food eaten on St. Valentine's Day in medieval times - plum shuttles, otherwise known as Valentine buns. Clearly tastes were simpler and purses lighter. It all began probably in medieval times when there was a strong belief that birds began to pair on February 14, so "Valentines" began in due course to wing their way into letter-boxes. Some may not realise that this year we mark Shrove Tuesday earlier in the same week, a day much more connected with food. The church bell rang for the priest to hear confession and give absolution, but post-Reformation it rather tended to prompt people to cook and enjoy themselves -

"But hark, I hear the pancake bell,
And fritters make a gallant smell;
The cooks are baking, frying, boyling,
Stewing, mincing, cutting, broyling..."

Shrove Tuesday and St. Valentine's Day link up also with the old custom of a single girl making a pancake and feeding it to the cock. The number of hens that joined him would be the number of years before she would marry.

"Men and maidens" may be stirring themselves but so also is Nature. Whilst rabbits are notoriously early starters of the breeding season, badgers can produce young in late February. There are signs of recent activity near me down our lane at a regular crossing-point. Brock insists on investigating the run and several badger "dung-pits" have appeared on the grass. A farmer friend in Hawkhurst has a sett on his farm and the badgers are engaged in frantic spring-cleaning; good housekeepers, they always carry out a complete change of nesting material.

Pheasants, now safe from guns, will also be able to give their minds to breeding. Some feel safe near houses and several friends have quite large numbers who regularly visit their gardens, or back doors even, for breakfast and corn. Among the numerous birds who visit my garden daily, I am always impressed by the patience and persistence of my chaffinches in their search for food; today, a full hour after the rest had gone, I watched four meticulously going over the feeding area for those tiny hidden seeds. Maybe it derives from their origin - finches in among the chaff of the stack?

In spite of the stiff south-wester today, we have enjoyed some mild sunny days and, on one such, I stopped the dog and listened - a thrush was singing joyfully. A symbol of Spring and Summer!

My Tuesday's "Daily Telegraph" carried a thoroughly encouraging photo. It was not of some protesting politician or a complainant in some sexual harassment case but of Robin Page, farmer, writer and presenter of "One Man and His Dog". He was smiling happily outside the BBC Television Centre, with a great sackful of 3,500 letters over his shoulder. One of them should have been from me and perhaps some of you wrote.

The BBC's proposal to phase out the programme has aroused a great deal of anger and passion. Heavy artillery is in support. Chris Smith, the Culture Secretary, is critical and Labour's backbench group of rural MPs has put down a Commons motion. The BBC naturally protests that they do not forget rural life, pointing to "Country File" and "Country Tracks" (shortly to return in July) and, on the radio, "Farming Today" and "Open Country". Nevertheless, there was something quite special about "One Man and His Dog". It represented, as well as anything could, the life and work and countryside of a great many farmers. It illustrated perfectly man and a fellow creature working in close harmony. Some of us may also sense, quite unconsciously, that the shepherd and his flock and dog are truly ancient. Moses and his large flocks must have had a dog or two; those shepherds near Bethlehem, drawn by that star, ditto, and probably the Romans on Romney Marsh, trying to contain the waters and introduce sheep to that wonderful grazing. Whether in Romney Marsh or the field behind my house, I cannot resist watching a shepherd working his dog.

When does Spring arrive? The calendar says "March", but February will sometimes whisper "Now", as it did yesterday the 23rd. As a good convalescent, I strolled slowly round Rolvenden Layne and studied the base of all the hedges, mainly frontages of gardens. The most common feature were innumerable clumps of those dark, glossy leaves of "lords and ladies", so often quite unrecognised by many passers-by as the earliest signs of new growth. In just one or two places I saw some of the hairy green leaves of cow parsley (visions of May and June!). In another, to my delight, three lesser celandines which will later turn the hedgebanks into a rash of yellow. But my special joy came from clusters of the common violet here and there, almost hidden under weeds and other greenery but, in spite of this, their deep violet proclaiming the first real colour of the hedgerow's new life.

In our gardens, of course, there are varied signs of Spring. In some, witch hazel, daphne and winter-flowering cherries are still displaying colour, but early japonicas often steal the show now. An orange-red one near me is a blaze of colour; another belonging to a friend has been fully out for three weeks. It seems likely that there will be no "February fill-dyke" this year - only about ¼ inch recorded in my gauge. I still find lambing synonymous with Spring and there is the sudden uplifting birdsong of both blackbird and song-thrush. I eagerly await the finding of a clutch of sky-blue eggs of the thrush, symbolic also of Spring itself.

Shrove Tuesday brought me an invitation to lunch and pancakes. It also brought the added pleasure of having beside me a simple arrangement of some iris stylosa and hazel catkins. Both speak to me of Spring and new life and colour. How exciting it has been, these past few days, to glimpse clusters of hazel catkins in most copses and woods, suddenly long enough to be caught by the winds and almost waving to the passers-by, hurrying to do shopping or to get home from work. Yet, other than bare branches, evergreen remains prominent in gardens and hedgerows, mainly yew and box and privet and laurel, with ivy clinging to any supporting neighbour. There is, near me, a slight change of colour on a willow shrub by a pond - that initial silvery-grey of its catkins.

A stiff south-westerly, with rain, is beating on my study window, as I write. It is not the first occasion of wind and rain this past week, yet the soggy wetness of our gardens and the verges is deceptive. Even if the ditches in my lane are full and there is standing water in the field, ponds are not at winter level and Bewl Water remains scarcely half full. We badly need the traditional "February fill-dyke". This stiff south-westerly nearly always stops my mallard from flying in; they prefer to lie low beside some sheltered pond. Yet immediately that there is a hard frost, they are back and ravenous. Last Saturday, after a break in attendance, they poured in - two flights of 12 and a few stragglers, all claiming hardship and starvation.

I venture to remind readers that, in spite of milder days at present, one should not stop feeding the birds. Natural food is still in short supply. They still need fuel to survive, especially the smaller garden birds. Most hedgerows have been picked bare. Twigs still harbour the occasional moth or butterfly egg. For certain birds there remains food in fields grazed by sheep or cows. Cow-pats, old or new, contain larvae and eggs, and sheep droppings in the field behind my house offer pickings to starlings and gulls and dunnocks. The gulls regularly appear at breakfast time for a conference mid-field and then disperse and spread out for foraging; by ten o'clock they are all gone, perhaps to a field being worked on the Rother Levels nearby.

It may not be gardening weather today but my seed order has arrived from Dobies, so I can dream a little. I have visions of a sprawling mass of nasturtiums, a bed filled with delicate pink godetias and a bowl of many coloured sweet peas in the middle of the table, filling the diningroom with their scent.

It is not easy to write a Country Article from one's bed, which is where I have been, off and on, for the last fortnight. So I apologise for a scrappy, unedifying article. First, of course, the view is different. All I can see is the top half of my elm and plenty of sky. This soon reminded me that numerous ordinary local birds make more use of wind currents than one realises. Most of us know and have watched, buzzards in the West Country or perhaps Scotland, hovering with wings angled against a high wind. Soaring and circling, they and eagles are adept and rivetting in their flight. Unexpectedly, I saw from my bed the local rooks and the occasional crow employing that technique in those South-Westerly winds we had a while ago.

On a rare walk down my lane ten days ago, I saw on a garden wall the first bluey-mauve flowers of an aubretia, in another garden, several iris reticulata and, in the next village, three pale iris stylosa by a front door - all three exciting signals of Spring. I believe that iris stylosa should be picked for the house, just as the buds show colour, and they will last for days. February Gold are usually the earliest daffodils, but each retirement year in Rolvenden, I have recorded the first clump of 20 ordinary daffs in flower on an open position exposed to all the wind and rain of the Levels in Lambsland Farm House garden. Single or double plants may be in individual gardens, but here, very early, by January 20th a large clump fully out.

Sick or not, I managed a quick visit to Romney Marsh ten days ago. My arrangements took me first to St. Augustine's Brookland (which was full of scaffolding and sheeting and dust) and then along that quiet lane to St. Thomas' Fairfield. Speed is down to 20 mph in order to absorb all the tiny things on the Marsh landscape. Patches of water here and there, mute swans in the distance, dykes all full and, to my delight, four or five small waders "trawling" in a dyke near the road, probably golden plovers, looking for worms and small shell-fish. The next day a friend told me of an invasion of those birds on Sheppey, between 15,000 and 20,000. What a sight!

MARCH

Last week some of us had our annual tilt at the Cruft's "windmill". There was a shade more humour and less ferocity than allegedly shown by Don Quixote. Secretly, most of us, dog-lover or not, are rather proud of having nurtured Cruft's, the largest and most important dog show in the world. Yet doubts linger as to whether all is well with its structure and its rules. So the Daily Telegraph Weekend displayed a front-page article headed "In praise of mongrels" and illustrated by a large photo of an alert tan and white head that was almost a border collie but not quite. The previous day "The Times" were even bolder, running a Third Leader allegedly written by "a Jack Russell". This was fame indeed for my favourite breed. They are favoured by the Monarchy, in the person of Prince Charles; they are favoured also by cabinet ministers and now they have won over the press in its highest echelon. What is left for them to conquer?

The "Jack Russell" writer enjoyed himself in all directions. Having first claimed a longer history than the Kennel Club, he then tilted at elitism, selective breeding and the average owner - "tweedy working breeds such as brigadiers and headmistresses" and called for three cheers for mongrels. Nevertheless, reading between the lines, one could not help but conclude that he was glad and relieved not to be among that highly-bred, over-groomed and conforming crowd. He would have been alarmed at the Cruft's Show results in Monday's "Times" - a Parson Jack Russell, named Cassacre Drummer, was classed as a winner in the Terrier and Hound Group. He would have queried his measurements and soon realised that he was neither "working" nor able to enter the smallest rabbit burrow.

As for myself, I enjoyed the coverage of the finals given to us by BBC2 on two successive evenings. We had brief glimpses of the judging, after each judge had summarized their methods. Interspersed and humorously presented was information about toys, food, handling and even bathing ("two pairs of hands are better than one"). There were other unrehearsed humorous moments, such as when the cameras had suddenly to be withdrawn from the unthinkable - three chihuahuas actually having a scrap. Thank goodness the cameras did not fail to reveal the really human side of the show - owner and dog having a snack and a snooze together in their partition, the bond of man and his best friend. There remained only for right-minded people to give thanks for Albert, the three year old cocker spaniel, named Supreme Champion. He will certainly know his way through wood and stream and at the end be able to recognise a pheasant.

We seem to be edging our way into Spring. The last pockets of snow in field corners have now gone. March has come in like a lamb, so it may go out like a lion. Hazel catkins are abundant and lengthy everywhere. Many a garden has had its clusters of snowdrops for a week or two and, in sheltered corners by front doors, japonicas are showing blobs of red to warm our hearts and our hopes. One such was by the door of an Old Romney farmhouse in the middle of Romney Marsh. But what claimed my admiration today was an amazing display of snowdrops in the spinney next to the house. Literally thousands were in flower in an area no bigger than 50 by 50 yards. Much ground ivy had been cleared in the late summer and the result was startling. Needless to say, the snowdrops had been long established and in World War II the farmer's wife had picked and sold hundreds of bunches in aid of those "Wings for Victory" weeks which stimulated the production of Spitfires and Wellingtons. Hearing this, my thoughts at once returned to Brookland church, my last call, where a leather-bound Prayer Book lays quietly on a small kneeling desk by the south chapel - inside it, this inscription -

"Presented to the Church of St. Augustine, Brookland, by an airman of World War II as a thank-offering for his safe return."

I wonder whether he flew Spitfires or Wellingtons. I wonder, too, whether we are forgetting the gracious virtue of being thankful and the precious heritage of our Book of Common Prayer. It was obviously one of the things that airman was prepared to die for.

Inside the farmhouse there was time for coffee and chat. How were the ewes? How were the young collies in training? Was there anything to report on the wildlife front? This held sway the longest. A pair of little owls had returned to nest (after a gap) but to everyone's sadness, one had been hit by a car this week. The robins, though, held centre-stage. Unusually, there were no less than four in the farmhouse garden. This seems to be more common; there would appear to be less fighting for territory and, only two months ago, another farmer friend in North Kent reported three robins in his garden and occasionally two on his bird-table at the same time. One of the Old

Romney quartet may be senior resident, as he has for a long period fed from the farmer's hand. More unexpectedly, he or another was fearless enough to perch on the lawn mower as it was moving.

Sometimes, of course, the appetite for good food can temporarily dispel fear of the human. An example of this occurred in our garden this week. A green woodpecker, having been twice disturbed by unsuspecting me, still returned a third time and spent a full half-hour, probing and boring into our small lawn, only three yards from the house. This female bird was a truly lovely specimen in full plumage, another example of Nature's unending beauty.

There has been a considerable change of scenery during the past week in both garden and countryside. The brown impression of woods and copses is now broken by the greens and yellows of hazel and willow catkins. Under foot is the advance guard of the wood anemone and the lesser celandine, many of which are lining the banks of verges. In our hedges are green patches of hawthorn in leaf. This heartening picture is reflected in our gardens. The daffodils and the eye-catching forsythia are out everywhere and so are the lawn mowers. Primulas of all colours are flowering prolifically in my own and neighbours' gardens, and so are the delicate iris stylosa plants in this area. A general picture of hope and expectation.

Small though my garden is, I am always expectant of the unusual bird. Suddenly, last week, it was there - a male reed bunting, on the flagstones near the garden shed. My surprise was two-fold; first, I am at least a mile from the nearest reeds and water and, secondly, I had read, only a week earlier, in my Daily Telegraph that the reed bunting is one of 36 birds on the "red list" of "high conservation concern". It stayed around for about half an hour, picking up seeds, and I felt privileged as well as excited.

Early on another morning that week I could have easily been on the quayside at Blakeney on the north Norfolk coast, given just a touch of imagination. I was feeding a trio of mallard at my feet when a pair of Canadas flew low over the house, honking loudly, to be followed immediately by the descent into the field of about 50 raucous, wailing gulls. In the near distance a flight of seven mallard circled neighbour, Jim's, water and a little further away there hung an early morning mist. It could easily have been hiding Blakeney Marshes and not the Rother Levels. The cry of a redshank would have clinched it.

I am having sparrow-trouble. They have been monopolising my nut container since the turn of the year, in spite of the RSPB advertising it as sparrow-proof. So I have at last taken the obvious action and last week hung up another ordinary nut container in another position in the garden; within half an hour, a blue tit was on it. Since then, green finches, recently missing from the garden, are again feeding here. It is a well-known tactic, I suppose, by anyone catering for a crowd to spread the food and reduce the competition and allow the less aggressive spirits (in this case the tits) more chance. Secondly, the house sparrows have been hanging round my house martin nests. It makes me very anxious. The "expected time of arrival" is soon, perhaps two weeks, and I want to welcome them to clean and unoccupied nests. It is a privilege to have these slim, sensitive migrants under one's eaves. Moreover, a report reached me through Rye Harbour watchers that a house martin had been seen ten days ago, also a swallow. A gamekeeper friend also claimed to have heard, with three others, a cuckoo in the Woodchurch area on March 14th.

The milder weather last week may begin to temp the early migrants, such as swallow, house martin and chiffchaff, but most readers will have noticed the blackthorn slowly coming out - flowers, now being joined by leaves. Within a day or two, the temperature has dropped and there has been a frost, all in keeping with the "blackthorn winter" of country lore.

The countryside generally is showing more colour. The brighter pussy willow is easily eclipsing the hazel catkins in hedges and copses. On ground level, wood anemones and celandines are carpeting most woods and roadsides, with the dark leaves of bluebells promising things to come. From my study window I can also enjoy the delicate pale green of neighbour Jim's weeping willows which invariably win the foliage race. Yet another colour is showing, here and there, rather shyly, in woods and on hedgebanks - the lilac blue of lady's smock and of the violet. The latter may be unscented and small but it is a contrast and linked traditionally to Mothering Sunday. In Victorian days, girls in service or on the farm enjoyed a holiday and walked home through the lanes, gathering a posy, often primroses and violets, for mother. Being Refreshment Sunday and a break in Lent austerity, there was usually a bit of feasting - perhaps roast veal and baked custard, with simnel cake and wafers for tea. It sounds an excellent day and a proper tribute to mother and family life. Nowadays it may have been hijacked by commercialism but it is, after all, emphasising a vital person in every individual's life. Few people know more about sacrificial love than mothers. May God bless them all in the weeks to come.

The field behind us was completely empty at 7 o'clock this morning. This is unusual. The ewes and their early lambs (the result of a break-in by an unauthorised ram) have recently gone down to the farm. Sheep or not, there are nearly always 50 or more gulls scattered evenly over the field on an early morning scavenge, often assisted by a few rooks and starlings. Often, too, a large greyish dog fox crosses the field, checking on the sheep troughs and the mallard and Canadas round neighbour Jim's ponds. A bonus these last few days has been a heron, statuesque in the middle and clearly wondering which way to go, with pieces of water in all directions. His method could be described as cautious and gradual - a couple of slow flaps of his big wings and then another look and think, sometimes interrupted by a jab

in the grass and a titbit of a beetle or mouse. Thus he gradually approaches Jim's water and lazily pulls himself over the hedge for the ultimate delicacy of a fish.

I cannot help but wonder where he comes from. I suspect that it may be Ashenden, near Smallhythe, one of the five major heronries in Kent, this one dating from 1915. At one stage in the 1950s and 1960s there was an interchange between Ashenden and Potman's Heath, even nearer to me, but the herons seem to have settled down over recent years at Ashenden. Nests there have already been refurbished and eggs possibly laid in some. Observation of heronries is never easy from the ground but in two cases in Kent details can be observed clearly. Lydd church tower offers a marvellous viewpoint for the small heronry in the Grange closeby, the home of the late Mr. Tim Paine, farmer, Baron of the Cinque Ports and Mayor of Lydd at least 35 times; sadly, the 1987 hurricane destroyed several major trees there and some of the heronry. Another good viewpoint is Lympne churchyard and church tower whence details of the large heronry in Lympne Wood can usually be seen at this time of the year. This longstanding heronry suffered a crisis some years after the War when marauding rooks established a rookery closeby in that wood and drove the herons away for a while through sheer noise and disturbance. Many owners of ponds, large or small, have a love-hate relationship with herons, but they really must expect the normal interlocking rhythms of Nature to operate at all times.

I was glad to learn that our village has again entered the Trees in Your Village competition. Some may not know of this admirable annual competition, now in its 25th year and run by the Kent branch of the Men of the Trees. The judging centres mainly round new tree-planting, the after-care of young trees and the care and appearance of trees in public places. Crockenhill, near Eynsford, the 1993 winner, was outstanding. The Parish Council had planted more than 1,000 trees on its land and also published a tree survey, containing maps, identifications and measurements of all the trees since the first survey in 1983. What an achievement! Moreover, I can personally vouch for the invaluable advice always given by the judge on his or her rounds. Trees so often bring relief to endless bricks and mortar and soften jagged outlines. Joyce Kilner, the poet, ascends to a higher level -

"I think that I shall never see
A poem lovely as a tree".

Even a short walk in the country can be interesting. Yesterday afternoon Brock and I chose Mounts Lane near me and, whilst he found a great many smells, I came across three seasonal "pointers". The first was a holly tree still laden with red berries, reminding me that the winter has been a moderate one, not continuous days of frost and hard ground. Germs have been plentiful in our daily round, but blackbirds, mistle-thrushes and fieldfares have not been desperate for food. A little further on, signalling that Spring had come, were numerous clusters of the common violet, with one paler wood dog violet, all shyly showing their beauty on a hedge-bank above a ditch. Another 100 yards and I had the tiny excitement of my first sighting of lady's smock, normally an April arrival. There they were, two stems, growing, as so often, in the base of a hedge; soon there will be hundreds of these flowers, on verge and hedge-banks, all over the Weald. These will be waiting for the orange-tip butterfly in early May to lay their eggs on their leaves.

Last Friday was also a moderately notable day. Three contrasting sights came my way. Passing Rolvenden cricket ground, I was delighted to see a grass-cutter on the edge of the "square". Groundsman, Tony Monk, had decided to do the initial cut, the beginning of another season. It only needed an elderly spectator to be sitting on the bench, waiting patiently! That same day the postman delivered the fixture-card of one of my cricket clubs - opening game v Bossingham, a North Downs village, standing on chalk; therefore, probably a hard wicket, unlike nearby Newenden, by the Rother, who can scarcely play at home in May. Later that morning I visited a friend and had to pause up the path. My eyes were drawn to at least 40 iris stylosa, all in flower below the bay window. Lovely to see so many together. Post-lunch, I was on my hands and knees, gently tidying my own beds in front of the house. Suddenly, hidden among the wallflowers, I saw a large brown egg, the size of a pullet's. A puzzle for my readers. Nobody keeps chickens anywhere near me. A knowledgeable friend wondered about a crow or rook, discarding its theft from a chicken-house or could it have been a passing springer spaniel, unsure what to do with an egg?

APRIL

Palm Sunday, not surprisingly, brings numerous donkeys out of their quiet pastures. They are needed to show their paces in village streets and, sometimes, in churches, as an integral part of processions on that special Sunday. This has not always been so, even though most congregations knew perfectly well that they were celebrating Christ's triumphal entry into Jerusalem "meek and sitting upon an ass". Comparatively recently, though, official sanction and encouragement has emerged in a printed service for Palm Sunday, actually mentioning donkeys and palms and local processions. So some clergy, remembering their oath of obedience to higher authority, are responding.

Staplehurst may claim to have done this for years, processing with donkey and palm-waving children round the inside of All Saints' church. A few years ago your scribe was heavily involved on that day in that church and found that the procession gave a sensible and joyful emphasis to the Palm Sunday theme - "All glory, laud and honour to thee, Redeemer, King..." I have to add that the donkey excelled itself; known to be a real veteran, there was doubt as to whether it would last the course. In fact it so enjoyed the music and the attention that it went round twice! This year I shared in the celebrations at Bethersden. The donkey was a veteran of fetes and functions as well as Palm Sundays and, in spite of or because of a suitably attired rider, went up the village street at a good walking pace which tested the choir quite a bit, trying to co-ordinate their music and their processing. I did happen to see one other donkey, walking sedately up Maytham Road towards St. Mary's, Rolvenden. Andora, as she is called, is 22 years of age and has this one day-out a year, so was understandably well-behaved. Just before Palm Sunday there came another more personal celebration. My friend, Ernie Lee, saw his first swallow, in fact five, over water near Coombe Farm, Tenterden on March 27th. I wonder if any reader can improve on that date? I cannot personally compete but I did quietly rejoice this morning, April 2nd, when I saw my first brimstone butterfly of the season. Somehow, its colouring matches up so well with Easter, the most joyful day of the Christian Year, and with the old country rhyme -

> At Easter let your clothes be new,
> Or else, be sure, you will it rue.

I am a trifle sad. My exhausted carrier pigeon which suddenly appeared on the 5th of March, seems to have departed, after a stay of nearly three weeks. He had become a friend, feeding among the collared doves, rooks and chaffinches each morning and usually spent each day on my roof. He obviously felt that he belonged and, last Sunday morning, when I was late feeding, he alone was perched meaningfully on my fence, obviously asking. I shall miss him, not least for his smart mushroom-pink body and pure white tail.

Still on the bird front, it is a period of coming and going. My nephew heard a chiffchaff for the first time on the 17th in the Cranbrook area, and yet another partial migrant, the fieldfare, was still very much present in numbers in my field a few days ago. We all now await the excitement of other summer visitors like the warblers and, of course, the cuckoo, the swallow and the housemartin. The last to arrive is usually the spotted flycatcher which often waits till May before re-occupying last year's nest in the fork of a climbing rose. My pullet's egg, found among my wallflowers, still sits on my desk, awaiting ideas!

Like many others, I hope, I enjoyed greatly, a week ago on Sunday, the BBC2's "Natural World" programme, quietly following the seasons on a North Devon farm, worked by traditional methods. The emphasis was on the wildlife that such methods create. Spring ploughing, wide field margins, uncut meadows and old barns produced a galaxy of birds and flowers - barn owls, kestrels, swallows, all nesting easily in the old buildings. Orchids, daisies and buttercups were prolific. The photography was excellent and the shots of the harvest mouse in its nest (with the reaper coming closer) were memorable. Full marks also to Jonathan Dimbleby for his commentary - sensitive, expert and limited. The plea was to everyone not just to drool over lovely countryside and wildlife but to be far more selective and demanding in their food shopping.

On all sides, garden and countryside, there is increasing colour. White and yellow are still predominant, but I have recently been conscious of blue infiltrating into the colour scheme, its style quiet and its exhibits small and scattered. The ubiquitous forget-me-not is present in most gardens and, in my own, is well supported by several clusters of anemone blanda (warmly recommended by Fred Whitsey in Weekend Telegraph); it seeds itself, loves the sun and offers such a clear blue. Spreading along my fence are increasing numbers of periwinkle flower. Protruding under numerous hedges in the village on all sides, grape hyacinths compete with yet more periwinkle for light and air.

But I still love to see a spreading bush of male pussy willow in full flower. This year it was ready and waiting for all those ladies who arranged flowers for Palm Sunday in their parish churches. Some churches also feature a donkey and a procession, singing St. Theodulph's magnificent hymn "All glory, laud and honour". I greatly enjoyed such a procession at Kilndown last Sunday. I am also reminded of another, a few years ago, in All Saints, Staplehurst. The donkey was old and might not last the circuit, I was told. In fact, the accompanying children and music so roused the animal that it insisted on two circuits.

A Happy Easter to you all!

Easter Monday found me planting my seed potatoes, theoretically three days late. I was not too worried. Many country people of my acquaintance scorn the Good Friday date; they often wait another month for the soil to have more sun and warmth and still produce the potato shoots just as quickly. In addition, it was a truly rural setting on my daughter's farm. The most obvious sound was a cuckoo calling, moving here and there among distant clumps of trees. Closeby on one side was a three day old kid, beautifully white and watched over by its mother, who was deeply suspicious of my Jack Russell trying to nuzzle its offspring through the sheep wire - so there was much stamping of feet. On the other side, Rhode Island Reds noisily proclaimed the laying of yet more eggs or continued automatically scratching for more insects in the dusty soil. In the Home Field, mothers called to their lambs straying further than they should.

As that day wore on, the breeze increased and by nightfall it was almost wintry. It is hardly surprising that the early butterflies have recently disappeared and the house martins have not returned to work on their nests under our eaves. Swallows have, however, been seen in the Hawkhurst and Sandhurst areas over the past week. Whilst I have scarcely seen a tortoiseshell for a week, I was delighted at least to catch a glimpse of my first orange-tip butterfly crossing a Rolvenden lane on April 12th.

On road verges and in woods the ground scene continues to give even more varied colour and pleasure to the eye. White dead-nettles and greater stitchwort have now joined the prolific primroses, lady's smock and celandines on the roadsides. In some woods the bluebells now offer a veritable sea of blue, as if hurriedly coming into flower before the leaf canopy overhead excludes the light. More Early Purple orchids have emerged since last week, rather earlier and more numerous than last year.

Scarcely a week goes by without the publication in our papers of yet another wildlife survey. Last week we read about the first national census of mammals and the Week-end Telegraph devoted a whole page to the skylark, written by Robin Page, well-known farmer-naturalist. These surveys are most welcome in that they inform and educate a vast public as well as the experts, but statistics can be made to prove anything and their figures should be treated cautiously. For instance, the Game Conservancy consider the estimate of foxes (240,000) by the Bristol University mammal census rather low, as well as that of the brown hare. Auberon Waugh, himself a landowner, questions in his weekly column the accuracy of the survey method, bearing in mind that he and other landowning friends have never filled in any questionnaire. Nevertheless, like Robin Page, most of us scarcely hear a skylark these days and mourn the loss of its song, once a certain feature of open fields in Spring and Summer. We all need to support the appropriate Societies in their ongoing campaign to encourage more sympathetic farming and reduce spraying.

Farmer or gardener, we all need also a half day's steady rain SOON. The ground has dried rock hard. April has brought scarcely 1 mm of rain here. What a contrast to the 62.5 mm of March!

A single red tulip has uplifted my life daily for the past week. It was one of a cluster in the herbaceous border and had seemed to be at the end of its life. So I brought it in and placed it in a specimen glass (with a few leafy stems of winter-jasmine) in my kitchen window. It responded with new life and its crimson glow filled the whole room, opening up a little by day and shyly revealing the contrasting dark centre, bordered with yellow. Four and a half inches in diameter, it was a truly lovely companion for my meals and equal to a glass of Chateauneuf du Pape. The pocket Oxford Dictionary defines crimson as "rich deep red, inclining to purple" and this is, I suspect, a little different from the brighter red of St. George, whose day it was last week. I hope he was widely remembered, with flags flying on churches and public buildings. Memories and associations with the saint live on and tumble over each other. I have the indelible memory of celebrating my first Holy Communion at the altar of St. George's Ivychurch, the cathedral of Romney Marsh. This year my house martins returned on April 23rd for their initial reconnaissance. That annual miracle, known only to God. Brock and I rejoiced quietly over breakfast.

It is a time of reawakening, countryside and wildlife. Cuckoos can be heard everywhere, marsh frogs on the Rother Levels have found their voices again for mating and at least two clutches of mallard have hatched out down our lane. Typical of the transforming scene has been the horse-chestnut, within a few days in full flower, its "candles" radiating both grace and grandeur. Behind all this, of course, has been the intensity of rain, alternating with sun.

Nearly four inches have been measured in my gauge this month and the mower has been in action three times. But usually the evenings have been calm and peaceful. From my first-floor study window, I watch the light, gently fading and leaving the skeletal trees of the wood across the field, silhouetted against a dull blue and amber sky. It speaks of peace, and there is joy closeby, too. It is half an hour before sunset and one of my blackbirds is singing in my elm. He is having a rest from feeding young

in the nest in the hedge. The hen has just flown from the same perch, her beak full of worms. A mother's work is never done.

The dawn chorus is, by repute, at its height and earliest in mid-summer. Traditionally, it is the skylark that begins it about 4 am. Nevertheless, even late April, I am aware in my sub-conscious state of an early chorus that follows roughly the same order each morning. Whether it hastens my wakening or not, I thank God for its intrinsic country character, as opposed to the subdued roar of traffic or one's neighbour's radio.

As there are no skylarks in the area, the first sound to register is usually the cock crowing in the field behind me. He is a magnificent Light Sussex cock and believes that we should wake up at 4.30 am. He is soon followed by the honking of the Canada geese on the water over the hedge; they invariably talk before flying off noisily to some nearby feeding-place. By this time the rooks at the Frensham Manor rookery are discussing loudly which field to visit first for breakfast. In the occasional silences I often hear the harsher, croaking "kraa" of a crow, repeated three times. By this time, it is 6 am and, now more awake than asleep, I am provoked into action by insistent and loud "quacking" below my window - my mallard want breakfast at once. Such is my April dawn chorus, a soothing, re-assuring introduction to another day in the country-side. There remains one small problem - how to get out of bed without upsetting Brock who always anticipates the chorus by curling up in the crook of my legs under the duvet.

Last week I referred to blackbirds, their increased numbers and uplifting song, in particular one bird down our lane. Remarkably, he is still there, on the wires, every morning (even though I vary the time somewhat) and singing beautifully. A reader from Robertsbridge is so concerned about the lack of earthworms for blackbirds in these hard conditions that she has just taken delivery of a consignment of live meal-worms and waxworms. Full marks to her, and she is prepared to go on through the summer, if necessary. Apple peelings are also always very acceptable to adult birds. Many species are very busy feeding their young and are often weary and slower, so I hope all motorists will be alert to lift their foot off the accelerator and thereby save those hedgerow-nesting birds.

Ironically, the new cricket season encountered rain last week-end. Rolvenden can-celled Saturday's game and only managed to play on Sunday because of their brand-new artificial wicket. Benenden, away at Biddenden, struggled to keep their feet, while getting wetter and wetter. Not good practice for Sunday's game in the opening round of the National Knock-out Competition. The 19th century giants, Edward Wenman and Richard Mills, would have carried Benenden through to the final, rain or no rain.

"One swallow does not make a summer" and how very accurate the old saying is this month and year. Single swallows have been reported locally since the start of April - Sandhurst on the 4th, Old Romney on the 9th and Rolvenden Layne on the 10th. Now, April 13th, six inches of snow and hail are banked up against my garage and the wind has changed from South West to North. One just hopes and prays that those early swallows are sheltering in the garden sheds and open barns where they love to nest. The few cuckoos already here must be glad of the woods that are so often their habitat. When seen on the wing, the cuckoo can easily be mistaken for a male sparrowhawk, and I am reminded of an incident two weeks ago. A countryman friend, recovering from hospital and an operation, had been greatly cheered by the regular singing of a blackbird in his garden. Visiting him, I found him on hands and knees searching a hedge. A sparrowhawk had swooped but the blackbird had just escaped and was recovering from the shock. Once again, he is singing but minus most of his tail feathers.

I wonder how many readers have made a simnel cake, or even know what it looks like? It is a splendid cake and my favourite of the year. Traditionally eaten on Mothering Sunday or Easter Day, mine reached the tea-table a few days late and was about to be cut in the presence of two neighbours, when I saw a queen wasp appear from nowhere and settle on the delectable marzipan, in fact on one of the "apostles". For the third time in two weeks, I had to eject a queen wasp.

Like many villages we have just held our Spring Flower Show. Having competed with extremes of weather, it had the further competition of the Grand National. Some gardeners had miraculously preserved a few unblemished daffodils; trumpet, large-cupped and double were all there but entries were down in number a little. Surprisingly, only two had entered the class for "An arrangement of spring flowers and foliage to be judged by popular vote". Surely this is within the compass of most housewives and not attracting the strict floral art criteria?

This column would not be complete without a very warm tribute to Frank Day whose thanksgiving/memorial service was held last week in Marden. St. Michael & All Angels was packed with his many friends and admirers. Farming, Cricket (County and local) and Village were all there in enormous numbers to support his family and give thanks to Almighty God for a wonderful example to everyone. The "grand old man" of Weald farming, Frank never looked old and, in spite of success, never changed. His great friend, Alan, gave a full and amusing tribute. Yet my chief thought throughout was of Frank (with Barbara) always in his pew there, Sunday by Sunday, or, if in Antigua, in his church out there. He understood completely the opening words of the last hymn we sang -

> We plough the fields, and scatter the good seed on the land,
> But it is fed and watered by God's almighty hand.

MAY

Each new day is a gift. The first sounds on awakening can also be a little precious and linger and perhaps set the mood for the day. Two days ago, the first conscious sound at 5 am was the singing of a blackbird, nowadays the acknowledged leader of the dawn chorus. The day before, it was the persistent honking of Canada geese, flighting over the Rother Levels closeby and always a little noisier at mating time. What handsome birds they are, too, when standing. Last week a pair arrived in our field on several successive mornings. They behaved as if on reconnaissance and tended to stay around two low piles of last year's hay - a possible nesting site? But they have not re-appeared since the farmer fertilised and rolled the field. This morning I awoke to a loud cawing; a Frensham Manor rook was perched in my elm, staring straight at my bedroom window. His message could have been "Wake up! I want some of that bird seed".

Yesterday, however, just out of bed and surveying the front of the house, I was intrigued to see one of our resident magpies searching for breakfast. He was boldly hopping in and out among the tables of the pub forecourt, looking for scraps from last night's diners. He then checked round the back near the kitchen entrance and the dustbins. Quite intelligent behaviour. Like gulls, magpies can be useful scavengers and this may divert them a little from robbery - of young birds and eggs. Nests and nestlings can be casualties from other creatures, as shown in a story reaching me from Bethersden. A householder, letting his spaniels out into the garden, was horrified to see them go straight for a blackbirds' nest in a bay tree and tear it down, two newborn chicks included. Owner and wife immediately lined a small wicker basket with the remains of the nest, put the fledglings inside and wired it to the tree. Within a short time, mother went back and the young are now growing feathers. Such success is extremely rare, no more than 1in10. Full marks to Mr. & Mrs. Storrer and mother blackbird.

The weather has been typically April, till last week, alternately sunny and showery. Friday night, brought an inch of rain in my gauge. It also brought snails out in great numbers; I found 20 surrounding an unplanted michaelmas daisy, standing in the middle of a seed tray. Marsh frogs have emerged from hibernation and are typically noisy in our local ponds, at this time of mating and spawning. Orange tips (male and female) have been on the wing in the midday sun along the lane verges and a well-marked speckled wood landed near me yesterday in a shady drive. The pleasure, though, that has uplifted me most is possibly the simplest - the annual carpet of bluebells in full flower in the woods near me and in particular in the grounds of Great Maytham Hall.

It has been a long wait since 18th of April 1997 but I have lived in hope. And then, unexpectedly, it happened. Seated at my study desk on Sunday evening, I saw a large bird coming across the fields in a direct line for my house. One of my mallards had remembered me and he lowered his "wheels" to land perfectly on my lawn. I almost fell downstairs in my joy and haste to feed him, a drake in shining plumage. He has flown in each day since, and twice yesterday. This was a case, surely, of memory, not instinct, like that of the house-martin to its nest. There is not the smallest pool in the garden but, ever since Angela and I arrived here in July 1990, mallard have visited regularly and in enormous numbers in the winter of 1996/97, anything between 30 and 50 in a day. Then suddenly they stopped. They had become friends, calling daily and I felt bereft. There was nothing I could do but hope and I had resolutely kept the canister of mixed corn ready in the kitchen all these months. Hope and, perhaps, a bit of faith in the mysterious workings of God's Creation.

The drake's return on Sunday also seemed to me rather appropriate, in that it was Rogation Sunday. On that day the Church by long tradition sings litanies and processes, asking God's blessing on the crops and farm animals and village life. The perambulations and prayers in Rolvenden had certainly included one stream, as well as hop gardens, orchards and sheep. We may be well fed but the Christians in the Sudan would certainly tune in to the opening words of the Collect - "O Lord, from whom all good things do come..."

Walking Brock on the Levels is sheer joy at present. The scents of oil seed rape and "may" dominate and compete with each other and challenge the eye on all sides. Orange-tips, male and female, were everywhere, suggesting a good hatch, and occasionally I put up a faded tortoiseshell and peacock resting on the track in the sun, survivors from hibernation. This week, too, I have seen my first dragon-flies, enjoying the sun and darting from one dyke to another. The fastest-flying and oldest insects in the world, perhaps 300 million years old. One's mind boggles.

Always, though, in a warm May, one's garden calls urgently and insistently. I think of the Summer Show on July 11th and then look at the herbaceous border. The double

paeonies are correctly offering their deep red flowers for Whit Sunday (in a week's time), the lupins are showing several spikes in colour and one delphinium already has a sky-blue spike; so, will any be in full flower by July? The roses are in flower now but, with careful dead-heading, might still be worth exhibiting mid-July. My best hope may be my sweet peas, planted later than usual. Dobie's "Bouquet Mixed" might be a winner.

The South of England, and especially Kent, are used to invaders. Usually they have two legs. I am particularly aware, at this moment of two species with four legs - the edible dormouse and the marsh frog. I have just watched the repeat of a delightful documentary by the BBC Wildlife Unit at Bristol about the edible or fat dormouse and each evening I hear the loud croaking of numerous marsh frogs in my neighbour Jim's garden. Both are introductions from Europe. The dormouse was brought by the eccentric zoologist, Lord Rothschild, to Tring Park in 1902 and the frog to a garden at Stone-in-Oxney, Kent, in 1935. Both are spreading, perhaps the dormouse more than the frog.

The tale of the edible dormouse was intriguing. Skilful photography and my favourite actress, Diana Rigg, told the story. If you live in the Tring-Beaconsfield area, you are liable to find these dormice in your loft or garden shed or copse. They might take over the tit-box in your garden or chew through the electric wiring of your house or vital connections in your Rolls-Royce. By further skilful photography and timing the Film Unit managed to show an edible dormouse investigating a labyrinth of organ pipes in a parish church, while the congregation were signing "All Things Bright and Beautiful"! For a wild animal they were surprisingly trusting. They did not seem to mind cameras or humans and were prepared to receive pieces of apple, almost from the hand, and to run up a man's arm, if the chance came. On the debit side, they are a pest out of doors as well as inside the house, damaging trees and sometimes plundering birds' nests. What to do with them, a protected species?

The marsh frog is an old friend to all of us who live near or on Romney Marsh. Each year, in this April-May period, they remind us that Spring is here once again. The loud croaking of the males in this mating season carries hundreds of yards on a still evening. Some years ago it was a regular and expected background noise to the coffee interval at the Ellen Terry Theatre at Smallhythe, as one strolled in the garden. Sadly it is no longer audible and, even more sadly, that unique theatre is in its last season. Later this month Roger Hume presents "Winston" a portrait by Allan Weedon. Maybe it is the right note to finish on. But for "Winston", life would have been very different for all of us, whether town or country dwellers. In those dark days of 1940 he roused us all, above all the Men of Kent, to get ready to repel many thousands of two-legged invaders. He echoed that battle cry of Edward III, centuries before, "St. George for England!".

My daily newspaper is, sadly, 75% about people behaving badly, either to one another or to society in general. It was a change and a pleasure to read the other day of quite a lot of people behaving well - towards an animal in danger of its life. Refugees are daily shown in distress on our TV screens but I found the photo of the terrier trapped in a storm drain even more distressing. It just showed one anxious eye and half an ear, plastered in slime down a ten foot hole in a road. It was an astonishing story. Having seen the dog disappear down the storm drain, its owner had somehow managed to follow its yelps and movements for almost a mile until the pipe joined a new drain under a new estate. The all-night rescue operation involved owner, family, villagers and building employees and digging up a new road! Heart-warming. They deserve a medal.

From domestic animal to the wild. An engaging story reached me the other day from a woodman friend working in a plantation of young trees. As he removed one of the many "tubes", used to protect and encourage growth, he suddenly saw a dormouse in a slight nest at the bottom. It immediately ran up George's trousers to his waist from where he picked it off and put it on the ground, for it only to climb ten feet up a nearby hazel, frightened and shocked. Basically, good news for Kent Wildlife and English Nature; rehabilitation schemes are underway in various Kent woodlands.

Good news also came from Hawkhurst farming friends. A pair of skylarks have returned to one of their fields of corn, after a ten year absence. Numbers remain low on Romney Marsh but are normal on my brother-in-law's farm in North West Scotland. Nightingales have recently been heard in two separate locations in Rolvenden. The cuckoos have gone rather silent in the prevailing breezy weather, and house martins are at least above and around Rolvenden Layne, doing lightning recces of our local nests.

The egg saga in the Layne continues. My own pullet's egg in the wallflowers four weeks ago (still unsolved) was followed, two weeks later, by a goose's egg half-buried in a friend's tub, and, last week, a near neighbour found a pheasant's egg in her front flower-bed. The mysterious disappearance of the large goose egg two days later could just have been the work of an animal, but the original placing of these eggs are rather more difficult to explain. Could a practical joker be hiding round the corner?

Maypole dancing and possibly madrigals are invariably linked with May. Both somehow express the spirit of the month - new life, vitality and joie de vivre. Country sayings on the subject abound but are cautionary rather than encouraging. We all know "Ne'er cast a clout till May is out" and most know "A

swarm of bees in May is worth a load of hay" but we tend to ignore "Marry in May, repent alway" and "A hot May makes for a full churchyard". This last is fairly relevant and Thomas Morley's famous madrigal -

> "Now is the month of maying
> When merry lads are playing, fa la..."

is also pleasantly topical. Thanks to the rain and, now, days of sun, our Wealden country-side could hardly look more lovely. Soothing to both eye and mind, as we move around - the cow parsley on the road verges, the "may" in full blossom in and above many hedges and, here and there, a horse-chestnut festooned with "candles", and all these against a universal background of fresh green foliage:

I suspect that the bird and insect worlds are also revelling in the warmth. Nests and families are appearing in unexpected places. To my delight, a page of my Daily Telegraph carried a heading "Mail service postponed as birds nest in letter-box" and a large photo of the pillar-box and a great tit about to enter. The Royal Mail had placed their prim official notice and the postman had put his - "Please use box in Thimble End Road"; and it all happened because the postal service had four days off at the Bank Holiday! What a pleasing change from endless news of posturing politicians and complaining individuals. Within 24 hours of this item, I opened a friend's office door and was shown another great tit's nest in that letter-box. I am reminded of swallows which nested on a wooden hay rake in my rectory garden shed and of robins which built their nest on the church mop, temporarily airing outside the porch.

Besides being opportunists, some birds sing beautifully and, in common with several friends, I am especially conscious of blackbirds. It is hard to better their rich, fluty warbling. Morning and evening one particular bird sings his heart out at the top of my elm and he does my spirit the world of good. He is barely twenty feet from where I sit at my desk. He brings me the joy and the companionship that I need.

The Chelsea Flower Show is with us once more. Worried exhibitors have been photographed, battling against persistent winds. My "Times" this morning displayed a striking photo of the "actress and the bishop", the delight of social folklore. Jane Asher was shown introducing the Bishop of Norwich to a new rose, launched to mark the 900th anniversary of the cathedral. It was such a happy study that few may have noticed the clash of colours - within a few inches of Jane Asher's lovely auburn hair was this pink rose, itself a few inches from the bishop's purple stock! With last summer's drought in mind, many exhibitors were emphasising plants and shrubs able to face a shortage of water. This was a reminder, surely, for us small gardeners, to keep our compost heaps in good working order or to start one, if there is none in our garden.

Last Saturday I found myself in "the Cathedral of Romney Marsh", St. George's Ivychurch, not quite so old as Norwich Cathedral but at least 600 years of age. The occasion was the Annual General Meeting of the Romney Marsh Historic Churches Trust and made more notable and crowded by the presence of the Duchess of Devonshire, writer, public speaker and chatelaine of Chatsworth. She spoke eloquently and amusingly and most of the 150 present forgot the cold of that grand 14th century building, calor gas heaters not withstanding. Having thanked the Duchess, President John Doyle reminded the audience that the church clock had just struck 3 o'clock. This would not continue, he said, unless at least £2,000 was found to overhaul its works. "Hands in pockets! Cheque books at the ready!"

It brought back memories. Once a week, for about three years, I had climbed that tower and wound the enormous clock handle. Someone had been doing that for 150 years and in World War II the Home Guard had climbed even higher, to the very top, to keep watch across the Marsh in those anxious but exciting days of 1940. Below them, in the north aisle, would have been the ARP and Fire Posts, continuing the tradition of the medieval church being the meeting-place and refuge for the community as well as for celebrating the Mass. Cromwell's men are also recorded as billeting themselves in the church.

If the stones of St. George's could speak, they would tell us of many things in these past 50 years of peace. They would tell us of drama and much music in the nave, of Harvest Thanksgivings and Suppers, of numerous christenings round the 15th century font and an occasional wedding. Above all, they would tell us of the regular worship of the faithful few in the 15th century choir stalls, offering themselves and the tiny community through the sacrament of Holy Communion.

JUNE

June is possibly the month most filled with scents in the countryside. It is almost impossible not to be aware of haymaking because of its pungent dusty smell, spreading well beyond the field concerned. Less strong and gentler is the scent of a field cut for silage. Or again, walking Brock up my road along the hedgerow, I became aware of a strong, not unpleasant smell in front of me and soon came level with a stretch of privet really covered in flower and, a few yards beyond, of hawthorn whose flowers had now given way to innumerable strands of honeysuckle, decorative and sweet-smelling. Being thick and cluttered with endless years of leafy accumulation, this hedge is a refuge for slugs and snails and, the evening before, we had disturbed a hedgehog snuffling happily along its base, enjoying the feed of a lifetime after some rain. It was perhaps Brock's first encounter with that mammal and he sensed danger as well as curiosity.

But, of course, the most widespread scent of June is from roses, so beloved of poets. Only last Sunday, after early Communion on the North Downs, I breakfasted in a panelled dining room to the scent of roses. A centrepiece arrangement of old-fashioned roses from a gracious old-fashioned garden lent refined contrast to sausages and bacon and croissants, as well as holding its own with one's olfactory organ. There was the additional pleasure of a brief tour of the garden, dignified and yet informal, grass walks, herbaceous borders and rambling roses and, above all, a magnificent Rambling Rector! There it was, of immense girth, round a dead hawthorn, and rising to over 20 feet high, completely covered with hundreds of white clusters of this single, delicate rose. All this had happened in barely six years. In our small garden we are delighted and rather proud of our latest planting, Octavia Hill, a floribunda produced after eight years of development by Harkness Rosegrowers to mark the Centenary Year of the National Trust. Its delicate pink bloom retains its compact shape longer than many roses and would suit admirably a large button-hole. In its first year, this fourth week of June, it is bearing 22 blooms. The growers maintain that this new rose would suit the original Octavia Hill who was "a lady ahead of her times, a social worker and philanthropist and one of the three founders of the National Trust".

Next year readers may see this rose in the garden of the Ellen Terry Theatre at Smallhythe. Stewarding at the theatre last week I was delighted to see and listen to the alternating musical and chattering song of a sedge warbler in the reeds closeby. It was a pleasant change from the raucous croaking of the marsh frogs that usually dominate that pool.

June brought me to a Kent village for my first wedding of the season. The church sat snugly in the middle of the village, surrounded by timber-framed houses which were overshadowed by a tall slim shingled steeple. The shingles hid a dangerous structure, I was told by a householder on its doorstep, so "no bells could be rung; my house would certainly be a casualty".

However, those in the church had the pleasure of listening to a competent young organist and, in due course, the further pleasure of an even younger choir from the University of London, who first led us through the traditional hymns "Love divine" and "Lead us..." at a spanking pace and then gave us two anthems during the signing of the registers. At the centre of the sacrament were Joanna and Bill, one English and the other New Zealander. They typified the enterprise and restlessness of the 90s - they had met on their travels, as usual by sheer chance, in a bar in the middle of Australia, in Alice Springs. So the exchange of vows brought a contrast in accents and a novel mistake by the Vicar, understandably nervous on his first wedding in that church. "Who giveth this man to be married to this woman?" he asked, and the whole congregation collapsed in laughter. He soon recovered and pronounced that "they be man and wife together..." and we all prayed with him that the Lord would "mercifully with his favour look upon them".

Out into the sunshine and to the bride's home for the reception. This entailed a long queue through the hall to the marquee on the lawn. On the way your scribe saw his first maybug of the season, quietly resting by the front door on an urn, containing splendid geraniums, possibly imported for the occasion. Where have all the maybugs been? Longing, I suspect, for some warm summer nights. Sparkling wine and hot sausages soon provoked conversation and bonhomie among the assembled guests, whether friends or strangers. The University singers added to the atmosphere with appropriate madrigals. John Farmer's "Fair Phyllis, sitting all alone..." was soon followed by Thomas Morley's famous madrigal "Now is the month of maying, when merry lads are playing, fa la!" In the distance, too, lay a wide swathe of may in dense flower, white and fragrant, the most prolific for years.

I love my garden. Small though it is, I find it daily absorbing and therapeutic but I wish I were more knowledgeable. Names elude me. This second week in June, my roses are dominant and prolific. Specially pleasing to my eye is Octavia Hill, in its third year and produced by Harkness to mark the National Trust Centenary. Its blush-pink flowers, perfectly formed, remind me of crinoline and Victorian elegance and charm. Also pleasing is my Rambling Rector, now in its second full year and beginning to ramble, in and among a white lilac, its tiny creamy-white flowers full of scent. I often wonder how that name came into the mind of the inventor? He must surely have known well a rector, probably a country rector, who rambled endlessly in conversation or sermons. John Betjeman, or was it Rupert Brooke, referred to portly rectors; they, however, conjure up visions of measured, weighty talk, with a glass of Chateauneuf du Pape beside them.

Some gardens possess other sources of scent this month. An example, often ignored, is privet. Near me is quite a long stretch of hedge (infrequently cut), covered with the fragrant white flowers, uplifting the senses of passers-by. Further on are two Portugal Laurels, their foliage drooping over the walker and festooned with dense, extremely fragrant spikes.

Even the hedgerows can compete with the gardens in June. Along every lane, the dog rose is in full flower, rambling happily in hedges and thickets and old willows along dykes. Similarly present in the Weald are masses of honeysuckle and everywhere, whether Weald or Romney Marsh, great clumps of elder are flowering prolifically. Most housewives know that elderflower cream is marvellous for the complexion. They also know, I hope, that elder has great healing properties. My Country Compendium recommends a "strong infusion made from dried elder blossom and flavoured with mint and sweetened with honey" as a cure for influenza. Most comprehensive cookery books include a recipe for elderflower water, good for stomach upsets and headaches.

On the weather front, gardeners, farmers and wildlife will all have been a little cheered - twice in a fortnight, over an inch of rain has fallen overnight in Rolvenden Layne, and other areas in the Weald have had further bursts of rain. The hay in the field behind me has been flattened but the blackbirds are once more pulling worms this morning out of my lawn.

Mothers naturally protect their young. In the wild it is frequent and yet always arresting, as with two recent cases. Opposite my house at 7.30am one morning, a black cat had somehow climbed a rear roof and was poised on the front guttering, less than a foot above a house martin's nest. The reaction of the adult birds was immediate and swift. They resembled rocket-firing typhoons swooping on some column of tanks and pulling out at the last second. My Jack Russell added his voice to my shouts and the "enemy" fled up the roof and over the other side. The other case was even more impressive. A female blackbird was facing a snake in a Newenden garden, presumably threatening its nest with young. With wings spread the bird fought the snake for a full ten minutes, its method being to spear its tail in quick jabs, gradually dragging it away from the nest until it was about ten yards away. This very courageous action was observed by friends who believed the snake to be an adder.

Many gardens are full of colour this half of June, especially those with herbaceous borders and climbing roses. Sometimes, too, gardeners are not afraid to include in their displays one or two semi-wild varieties. The owner of a gorgeous garden in north Kent, soon to be open to the public, had numerous foxgloves growing in selected places in her lovely herbaceous beds. Besides foxgloves, our own garden, like others in the vicinity, has several of the semi-wild great mullein or aaron's rod. This year, though, we found them covered with the caterpillars of the mullein moth, which must have been very busy laying a lot of eggs. Owners of buddleia, beware! These caterpillars, a little similar to those of the large white, also enjoy that plant, which is so popular later in the summer with the second brood of tortoiseshells and peacocks.

Village industries are, I believe, gradually increasing. One such is Crusty's of Staplehurst, reversing the trend. A hundred year old baking oven has been refurbished and modernised with gas-firing, after a gap of 40 years. The village bakery is in action again and doing increasing trade. Loaves of all shapes and sizes are emerging, together with the usual appetising smell. Their mini cottage loaf is just right for a ploughman's'. Well done, Mrs. Warren and family! Messrs. Kemp & Sons of Stepney, makers of the oven, would undoubtedly approve, as would Mr. S. Dunn, seen in an old print delivering bread from there in a horse and trap early this century. Personal service and the village craftsman are among the pleasures of the "good life".

It was 6.15 am on Ascension Day. A black cat greeted me warmly at the church door. A happy omen. Soon others arrived and, slightly breathless but exhilarated, about 20 of us assembled on top of All Saints Staplehurst tower. It was a lovely clear morning, so robed choir and others easily sang "Hail the day that sees Him rise" before descending to join in the Sacrament in St. George's chapel, followed by an excellent breakfast (egg, bacon and everything). Such was the tradition going back to the days before ordnance survey maps. From the 8th century, the elders of the parish, accompanied by the younger generation, walked the boundaries on the three Rogation Days before Ascension Day. In some parishes, where the land was flat, the children were taken on that day to the top of the church tower to have the boundaries shown to them. Four or five young children maintained that tradition last Thursday.

The next morning my rain gauge measured 9mm (over $\frac{1}{4}$ inch) and the morning after 12mm ($\frac{1}{2}$ inch). So hops grew 15 inches in the night and along hedges and dykes the dog rose and the elder rapidly come into flower everywhere. Do not forget the healing and refreshing qualities of elderflower water, ranging from stomach upsets and

headaches to a clear skin, an antidote to insect bites and sheer refreshment. Any good recipe book would guide you.

The nightingales seem to be in full song in many places and may often be heard by day in quiet periods. One or two cuckoos are already "changing their tune". Red admirals and peacocks seen around in the sun are still those who hibernated and are struggling on, battered and a little torn. On the other hand, the holly blues around have passed the winter as chrysalis attached to an ivy or holly leaf. The females are now active laying their eggs on the underside of these leaves, eventually to emerge as the second flight of butterflies in July or August.

It needed little imagination to sense tradition yesterday. Umpiring Newenden Present v. Past I enjoyed yet again the traditional village setting in lovely warm sunshine. Church and pub looked on, the steam train whistled and puffed into Northiam station and the commentator at Gate Court Farm could be heard extolling the virtues of the old working horses. With eyes closed, one could be transported back easily 70 years (but for the roar of passing traffic). From there it needed just a quick mental flip to imagine King Edward I staying at Lossenham, hunting and fishing. Above all, his wardrobe accounts contain the earliest reference to cricket, Newenden's special niche in the annals of our national game.

S tatues can lend character and dignity to a garden. Yesterday, my coffee with friends was enjoyed on a garden seat, with a statue of Hebe immediately behind us. It enhanced my coffee but Hebe being not only the goddess of youth but also cup-bearer to the gods, I also half-expected her to say over my shoulder "Would you prefer wine?"!

In front of us lay the lawn and a broad herbaceous border with numerous delphiniums, the queen of the border, prominent. In between on the grass, a pied wagtail bobbed up and down and regularly flew back to its nest, deep in a thick, tangled clematis on the garage roof. It is a normal site for them, helped foodwise by being alongside a farm with occasional stock and manure. Plenty of insects.

I daily see a pied wagtail on the wires by my house or on my lawn but have yet to locate a nest. Normally choosing a cavity or ledge in a wall, they have been known to build on the mudguard of a car, regularly parked outside a school. As we all know, small birds can choose extraordinary places for nesting. Last year, I remember, great tits took advantage of a Bank Holiday week-end and built in a pillar-box; the Royal Mail humanely directed customers elsewhere. A Rolvenden housewife has recently found that one of her lovely hanging-baskets had attracted a wren's nest. An awful dilemma. How to keep the plants alive and yet not soak nest and young?

My own house martins are feeding young but some from other nests may have flown. Only last week-end, there seemed to be five young martins playing like children in and above puddles down my lane. There are not many puddles around at present. The rain in the Weald has been very local - a torrential downpour in Biddenden four days ago left Tenterden bone dry. My rain gauge has totalled 28.5mm, almost all in the first week of the month.

I finish with feedback from earlier articles. My saga of the three eggs found near three front doors last month has resulted in a fair consensus of opinion. A fox is the most likely answer. "Charlie's" practice is normally to bury an egg and one was indeed buried; the other two were well-hidden in flower borders, which might meet the criteria. Secondly, hobbies are more numerous in Kent and East Sussex than I had realised. Another fishing friend enjoys their company (in fact, two pairs) when fishing near Sedlescombe. Even more impressive is a top count of 18 this Spring on a Romney Marsh Reserve nurtured by my friend, Philip Merricks. Great news, but not necessarily for smaller birds in the area, such as swallows and martins, which can be their secondary food.

In these days of noise and rush, it would seem good for all of us to enter, even briefly, the quiet, gentle, delicate world of butterflies and moths. I did just that yesterday. About to turn on a tap on the bathroom basin, I suddenly saw a dark brown moth (perhaps a chestnut or a quaker), motionless under the tap and semi-waterlogged. I gently levered this wet insect onto an envelope and slowly transferred it onto the bath-mat on the side of the bath. An hour later it had gone, flown off. Rather satisfying. As some may know, the resilience of moths, daddy longlegs and other frail insects, suddenly immersed in water, can be amazing. Many is the time in mid-summer and lying in one's bath that I have baled out suicidal creatures, usually with a scallop shell that is always handy.

In general, though, the nights have not been warm enough to bring the night-flying moths round our windows. The butterfly world has been noticeably absent, too. Heavy showers, breezes and occasional bursts of sunshine will not have helped their breeding in April and May and must have deterred any survivors from taking the wing. A few speckled woods were around in early May. So far no signs of red admirals or even meadow browns, our commonest butterfly and prepared to fly in both dull weather and sunshine in the hayfields and hedgerows. A few tortoiseshells from the May hatch should soon be on the wing if we have a few consecutive days of sun.

This leads me in thought to a friend's tale of his fishing this week on a piece of water not far from Ashford. He had the good fortune to observe the one hawk that feeds on insects. A hobby was trawling above the water for dragon and damsel flies, "almost lazily" he said; no lightning swoop that one associates with hawks. With only about 70 pairs of hobbies in the UK, it is a privilege to see one. Other friends from Goudhurst have had a pair of kestrels nesting in their garden; having already reared one chick, the birds are now busy feeding another, perhaps three weeks after the first one hatched, now flown.

JULY

July must rank as the month most full of English tradition. Wimbledon and Henley spill over into this month from "flaming" June, often alongside the University Cricket Match at Lord's. Nevertheless, for rural England, tradition tends to revolve rather more round the Vicarage fete and the Summer Flower Show. The latter came our way in Rolvenden last week and it was quietly enjoyable and local. Sweet peas and roses were there in fair quantity but only one delphinium entry, due to the erratic stormy weather in recent weeks. The retired head gardener (non-competing) was there, running a critical but kindly eye over the exhibits; pensioners, also non-competing, enjoyed the cups of tea and the company, one or two busy housewives ran off with the medals and a cup and small children squeaked with delight over their table of exhibits. The latter represented miniature gardens on a plate or portrayed a dubious species of butterfly. At least one member had been up to the Hampton Court Flower Show but she might have got greater pleasure from the sight of her grandson, aged two, walking up to receive a prize for his "garden".

The day before, we had had the unusual pleasure of the Mayor of Ashford's Garden Party in our parish. The setting was Great Maytham Hall, formal, handsome and traditional, with spacious, lovely gardens to match, all designed by Sir Edwin Lutyens. Several hundred guests basked in the slowly emerging sunshine and enjoyed the usual ingredients of marquee, strawberries and cream and a brass band. Mayors and ex-Mayors mingled with Council officials, farmers, clergy and many local friends. Conversation at our table was not about Mrs. X's dress or local politics but embraced food in Provence, a rookery in a cherry orchard, archaeological excavations in Lincolnshire and hay making. Then came some promenading, including, of course, the old walled rose garden of the original Georgian house, made famous by Frances Hodgson Burnett in her story "The Secret Garden". Nowadays also, colourful but dignified herbaceous borders frame beautifully kept lawns. With this grand house looking down upon us the atmosphere was distinctly Edwardian and some guests, including my wife, had dressed accordingly. Another portrayed delightfully the 1920s era of the Right Hon. H.J. Tennant. He almost certainly employed a dozen gardeners. Today, these gardens, open weekly to the public, are maintained to the present high standard by two part-time lady gardeners, supported by two part-time men including the all-important charioteer on the lawn-mower.

July seems to have become the most crowded month of the year. Maybe it is now regarded as the safest month weatherwise. So village flower shows, Church festivals, garden open days, Fetes and private barbecues follow each other (or coincide) in headlong succession. One needs stamina as well as zest for life to enjoy the July calendar. One certainly needs both to enjoy the modern County Show and once again I tested those qualities at Detling last week.

The Kent County Show seems to become bigger and more crowded and more noisier each year. A tactical plan is vital from the moment of arrival. First call for me was the Flower Show, an enormous marquee full of floral displays and trade stands, at 9.30 am not too crowded and thankfully lacking the restless parties of schoolchildren. I soon found the two sweet pea specialists - Diane Sewell and S. & N. Brackley. Selection is easy. The displays are clearly labelled and the seed packets are closeby. New on Brackley's were Lucy (pink on cream) and Rosina (lavendar). On Diane Sewell's, Charlie's Angel (pale blue) and Lizbeth (deep salmon pink) were new to me. On now to the Cherry and Soft Fruit tent and a welcome from my friend and chairman, William Wakeley, himself a prize-winner for his Sunburst cherries. He tells me that cherries, helped by new varieties, are staging a comeback in the public's mind. From there, it was but a step to the Cornwallis building and enormous sleek Charolais and Friesian bulls that would need a crane to lift them. Visitors of all ages stare at them with wonder and awe in their eyes.

However, it was the Sheep Lines that were the rear oasis of peace and quiet; they do not attract visitors other than those involved in sheep and truly interested. Nevertheless, under the surface there was considerable excitement. The Romney Sheep Breeders' Society are celebrating their centenary this year, so the breeders were there in force. I was delighted to meet briefly Hugh Skinner who, with his wife Pauline, farms at Sissinghurst and runs the Society with great enthusiasm. Also present was George Horne of Westwell who claims to have Britain's oldest pedigree flock of sheep. His flock dates back more than 370 years and are surely worthy descendants of the animals brought to the Romney Marshes by the Romans. No wonder there is a great gathering of breeders and others at his farm on Saturday. Romney Marsh and its sheep are quite special to Britain.

The Customs and Excise were also there to reassure the public with their highly successful Search Dog Section from Dover; two Oxfordshire farmers were wooing

Kent farmers to consider rearing ostriches, but the Terrier Roadshow Racing team drew the largest crowd that morning; I could not help but admire Adrian Francis' patter but not necessarily his kilt. On my way out I was halted in my tracks by a truly delightful quartet playing at the bandstand. Double bass, guitar, trombone and keyboard, they were immaculately dressed as for the 1920s - white tie, monocle, carnation button-hole - and playing the Charleston. The crowd loved it. The quartet would have been at home in the old Criterion and I half expected Bertie Wooster to walk round the corner.

A s is well-known, bats are inclined to favour churches. The last fortnight has amply confirmed this. Only yesterday I found a churchwarden in St. Clement's Old Romney, busily engaged, with dustpan and brush, sweeping up bat droppings. They were right beside the Rector's stall and one hoped that he or his service book did not suffer any direct hits during Morning or Evening Prayer. Two days earlier I was summoned "with haste" (as St. Mark says of Herodias' daughter) to St. Mary's Rolvenden to deal with a pipistrelle, recumbent but alive on the vestry floor. What to do? Short of climbing up into the roof, I could only pick it up and take it outside and introduce it to a suitable habitat. Fortunately it was there, just outside the vestry door - a really thick growth of ivy on a buttress. The bat responded by snuggling further into the growth. It could still breathe the ecclesiastical atmosphere.

A week earlier, one of a party I was leading round some Marsh churches nearly sat on a bat in the 15th century choir stalls of St. George's Ivychurch. I was not in the least surprised. One could justifiably say that the church's history is steeped in bats! Over my own 50 years of contact with the church I have never known it to be without bats. My wife swept the church every week and their copious droppings were the main contents of her dustpan. A few years after we left the rectory, a successor, perhaps unwisely, decided to deal with the bats, once and for all. The whole of that grand lofty church was fumigated and the doors locked for several weeks. Needless to say, it did not succeed; the bats soon resumed their flutterings in the dusk. They have a long tradition to keep up, certainly in that church. There is an authenticated story of an Archdeacon in Victorian times making his annual visitation to Ivychurch. As he entered by the heavy west door, something fell on his head - a stuffed owl, placed on a beam to scare the bats. Startled by the impact, he naturally looked up and immediately saw an oval textboard above him, proclaiming the well-known verse from Genesis 28 "How dreadful is this place! This is none other but the house of God, and this is the gate of heaven." A reminder to him and everyone that a little fear and a little mystery are needed to give depth to the joy of worship.

M idsummer's Day, also St. John's Day, certainly left its mark on our countryside. We all basked, literally or metaphorically, in the sun and the warmth and then, suddenly, at the end of the day, came the storm. Tropical in nature, it swiftly blotted out the summer evening light and burst upon us. Patio supper parties ran for the house, branches crashed across roads, strawberry "tunnels" were torn from their moorings and gardeners watched helplessly from their windows. Some people were able to carry on; the marquee housing the diners and dancers of Benenden Hospital's Annual Ball held firm and the audience for the musical recital in Goudhurst Parish Church arrived barely five minutes before the rain descended.

Like many gardeners, I emerged fearfully next morning to inspect the damage. My anxiety centred upon my sweet peas growing up bamboos arranged as two "wigwams". One was flat on the ground and the other, halfway. By some miracle none of the 25 plants had been uprooted. Dare I claim a little credit for this, in that the "ties" were loose enough to allow some movement or even to yield to the violence and undo themselves? Delphinium and rose growers must have fared worse, as their plants were in flower. All gardeners and farmers desperately need to be philosophical. As I write, the weather seems to have settled down, temperatures have been in the 70s and haymaking is going on all around me. There has been a big hatch of meadow brown butterflies and readers must have seen them in hayfields, grassy slopes and verges in the past week or so. If this warm weather continues, they should be joined by the first brood of tortoiseshells, which tend to lie around in any sunny spot. Also on the wing soon should be the gatekeepers, sometimes called small meadow browns; they are specially attracted to bramble flowers which are rapidly multiplying in the hedgerows.

Moving into the wider countryside, one is inclined to think that, in spite of the erratic short-term weather, our current climate is much liked by numerous wild flowers. Many observers remarked how prolific the bluebells were this Spring and now I am moved to record what a very good year it has been for the common spotted orchid. Numbers have increased at almost all the regular sites. One lovely one in an open copse of a large garden displayed at least 100 spikes, as against a mere 20 last year. Though not strictly a wild plant, the Portugal Laurel has caught my eye again and again this past fortnight. Several gardens in the Rolvenden area have allowed it to grow into a beautiful ornamental tree and its long drooping creamy-white flowers are gracefully pleasing and full of scent.

To finish with a touch of humour, hitherto lacking in this article. Magpies are commonly regarded as merciless marauders and excite our wrath. Such was the attitude of a neighbour towards three "regulars" in his garden, until one day he had to laugh. One of them, obviously hungry, had decided that he wanted the cat's food outside the back door and, grasping, the cat's tail dragged it away. Astonishment probably deprived the cat of its natural reaction.

Sadly, we are past mid-summer's day, but the evenings are still long and light and leisurely. Mercifully, most people have stopped rushing about and there is a measure of quiet and stillness. From my upstairs study window, there is a min-

imum of movement - just a tremor from the elm leaves, a hot-air balloon hovers high overhead, a barn owl has just "quartered" the wood boundary and my house martins circle the field occasionally, otherwise stillness.

I have been all day in Romney Marsh, guiding a responsive party of people round some churches and, having been warmly greeted by Brock, I have spent an hour in the garden. There is a tiny bit of crisis in the air. The local Summer Show is in ten days' time and we've all had an erratic spell of wind, rain and sun these last two weeks, so what will be presentable, if anything? The roses, my pride and joy, are struggling on and I dead-head assiduously and hopefully. I watch my "Giant Pacific" delphiniums, almost in fear and dread; the spikes are a little too far advanced if the sun shines for more than two or three days before July 11th. But I need the sun so badly for my sweet pea plants, and a few warm nights as well. The traditional dilemma of the gardener.

So I give up and look back over the day. On our winding open road to Fairfield church, we disturb a kestrel, quietly waiting and watching for small mammals on the edge of the corn, acres of it. At Fairfield, we revert to real marsh - acres of pasture and dyke and hundreds of sheep, newly shorn and almost pristine white. In that state, the ewes seemed scarcely bigger than their lambs. In the foreground, this most romantic of all the Marsh churches, diminutive and dumpy, with its red and blue brick walls, historically rising out of the waters, "almost organic", as my co-lecturer said. Inside, I recall clearly once celebrating the sacrament in the tiniest of Laudian sanctuaries (no room for a server and scarcely space to genuflect). An experience. I recall, too, a memorable Confirmation there, a packed church, people standing and the Bishop of Dover tuning in so sensitively to the occasion. All the service a redshank was calling and, at the end, by sheer chance, the bishop with his crook led the whole congregation back along the causeway to the road. A wonderful pastoral photograph that was never taken.

We moved on to the other extreme - All Saints, Lydd, a cathedral, with a grand tower from which one can view the nearby heronry and the whole Marsh. Thomas Stanley of Canterbury built it for £280. Entering, one could not help but feel small, one's eyes instantly drawn to the powerful east window. The three lancets glowed with reds and blues, its theme, the offering of man's homage to his Saviour and Lord. Please God, it spoke for all of us.

A nation of shopkeepers or not, I think we could also claim to be a nation of gardeners. How else could the increasing number of Garden Centres flourish? Therefore, the number one enemy at present are slugs and snails. On all sides, there is wringing of hands and gnashing of teeth. People have gone away for a week to find their petunias a medley of lifeless stalks. They try watering their sweet peas and the spout of the watering-can is blocked by a snail. A Hawkhurst friend found snails at the top of her currant bushes and, another day, snails had surmounted windows of several feet high and entered the house. All this, presumably the consequence of our increased rainfall. The only consolation is that thrushes are generally increasing and they do so love snails!

Thrushes and blackbirds and chaffinches all seem to have had a good breeding summer. This very morning, as I looked out at 6 am, a young blackbird greeted me, looking slightly comical without a tail, but he obviously knew that the early bird catches the worm. My young house martins are already zooming around after insects and then crowding into or around their nests at night. Sometimes, overcrowding leads to ejection and one fledgling was found in a friend's garden; the only hope was that the parents might feed it on a window-sill. Another different sort of casualty was a young and apparently lifeless daddy longlegs in a saucepan of water in the kitchen. I gently scooped it out onto the cill and went upstairs to shave. On my return it had dried out and was flapping around normally. The resilience of insects is remarkable. More than once, I have rescued a moth from my bath water and it has recovered.

Although approaching mid-July, our roadsides are still lush and varied. Cow parsley has been succeeded by hemlock and hemlock is now giving way to patches of pink willow-herb and a rash of mugwort, tall and willowy. Diabetics and rheumatics used to value tea made from its leaves. In many hedges the dog-rose is still flowering happily and is now being joined by blackberries emerging in flower on all sides.

But my chief joy at present is the hay-field behind me. Cut three days ago, it has just been turned. Nothing is to me more traditional of the English farming scene than hay-making. John Constable was inspired to paint perhaps his most famous picture "The Hay Wain". Hay brings that exciting evocative smell. It brings back memories of family and friends all working together to beat the weather, and this may well happen behind me in a day or so. Even country rectors made hay from their paddocks; the old wooden hay-rake, that Angela and I used, still looks at me wistfully in my garden shed.

AUGUST

It was Lammas Day and the wedding of a niece in rural Norfolk. What better way to begin the month of August? As I turned the corner on my initial reconnaissance of St. John the Baptist, Morningthorpe, I saw to my delight a round flint tower, virtually unchanged since it was built in Saxon times. An architectural gem. Round it, in this quiet lane, were tall trees and dignified houses, including a vast Manor House, with pheasants sidling through its main gates and a pink-decorated Old Rectory behind the traditional cedar. Doves cooed, dogs barked and the nearby Church Farm was clearly "working" and up to date, with a long shed enclosing rows of lamps that might have been keeping young turkeys warm.

Returning later, one hour before the wedding, I found the doors wide open (a pleasant change from the locked churches in Kent), the lights on and a prominent notice "We welcome all ages, young and old, to this church". Nearby, the visitors' book lay open and two entries caught my eye. Two visitors from Denmark had written "It is a nice little church" and had then drawn a picture of their own. Two others, Philip and Jean Read of Harpenden, had added, rather movingly, "our great grandparents were married here on April 21st, 1834". Another sign of those stable times, based on a simple Faith, was a Victorian window to the memory of Samuel and Emily Westgate, "who attended this church for 50 years". It is a rarity nowadays, although I do know one country churchwarden who has served for over 50 years, archdeacons not withstanding.

So eventually to the wedding itself, traditional and Prayer-Book. A packed church and the bridegroom (in kilt) welcomed the bride, still very erect and slim from her days as a model. Supporting her were bridesmaids and page boy and, unusually, her dog. One could not fault her, a large rough-haired mongrel; she lay down quietly by the choir stalls and neither barked, whimpered or moved. One hoped and prayed that she also would help cement those wonderful words of the service "For better for worse, for richer for poorer, in sickness and in health..". A vision of dogs and children enriching family life. So we moved through the familiar words to finish with "Praise my soul, the King of Heaven" and Jeremiah Clarke's Trumpet Voluntary. Left behind on the altar was a "posy" of newly-cut corn, a symbol of the Lammas loaf. I ventured to suggest in my address that all marriages would be happier and longer if they were imbued with the spirit of Lammas, daily thanksgiving for the simple, basic things of life.

Lammas Day, 1st August, is traditionally the day for the offering of a loaf made from the first fruits of the new grain harvest. Yet, on the very next day, I saw no less than three tractors ploughing within a mile of St. Mary in the Marsh church, a sign of the changing times. Stubble, seeds and weeds had been there probably for no more than 48 hours. Efficient farming, allied to fine weather, had decreed that natural food for partridge, rook, skylark and lapwing had been ploughed in before they had had a chance to benefit from it. Gulls were certainly following the ploughs, picking up wireworms, leatherjackets and earth worms but they, being scavengers, have the choice of a much wider menu and do not depend on those special foods.

Some fields of wheat in this area have not yet been combined and Oliver and I regularly follow a footpath alongside and through one such field, my fingertips brushing the ears. Somehow I immediately feel very biblical and slip mentally into the occasion recorded by all three Evangelists. Christ, we are told, went on one Sabbath through the cornfields "and his disciples were hungry and began to pluck the ears of corn and to eat," literally living from hand to mouth. Thank God, most of us are spared that these days. We can also refer to Richard Mabey's book "Food for Free" and comb the hedgerows.

In these recent high temperatures and continuous sunshine, our mauve buddleia spikes are having a short life. Nevertheless, they have been crowded in the past two weeks, red admirals, tortoiseshells, peacocks, large whites and a few painted ladies all restlessly "imbibing" the strongly scented flowers. Whatever the books may say, I have yet to be convinced that the white buddleia has the same attraction. One bush near me had not a single bee or butterfly in midday sunshine yesterday. With the buddleias soon fading away, the bees and the butterflies will naturally seek other flowers and gardens with tobacco plants, lavender and mignonette will be popular. Besides nectar and scent, butterflies are also drawn towards certain colours; purple and yellow appear to be the most popular, with pink and reddish mauve the next. I think that observation of your garden over a period will confirm that in general they prefer light and medium shades to dark.

My week was completed by a truly English country wedding at St. Peter's Newenden, with the reception in a marquee on the shores of Bewl Water. However, there was an E.E.C. element present - an English girl was marrying a Danish boy, and

one could not help but wonder if the Vikings ever sailed up the River Rother, just across the cricket ground, and carried away a few attractive English girls! Inevitably there were numerous tall blond boys and girls present from that land and certain Danish customs crept into the reception. Warned by tinkling glasses, we roared approval of the bride and groom twice kissing publicly and avidly. Between the main course and the sweet, all "unmarried" Danes were urged on by the chief usher to kiss the bride - with the groom out of the marquee, and vice-versa between the sweet and the coffee. Oblivious of the lovely hats, the excellent menu, the music and the fun, a solitary fisherman sat below us in his boat, waiting patiently for that tug on his line.

Tractors and trailers, loaded with large round bales of straw, have been regularly roaring by for the last week. It is a reassuring sight. It also leaves behind a pleasing debris of straw along our fence and curb. Thank goodness the mechanical road-sweeper has been and gone a while ago, and we can enjoy this seasonal litter (strictly "bedding for beasts" according to the Oxford Dictionary) till wind and rain carry it away into remote corners or open gardens. Sadly, other things intrude. A few houses up in the road was an empty beer bottle, a danger to drivers and animals. Even further along was an empty "Autumn Gold" cider can by the entrance to a public footpath. Yet in neither case had anyone, walkers or nearby householders, removed them. This is sad. These two articles had been there for at least two days. Was there no community pride? Trying to set an example that day, I also gathered up five wrappings and a Coke can to add to my dustbin!

For the past week it has been either VJ Day or the hot summer as a daily feature in our newspapers. Last Saturday "The Times" letters devoted a whole column to the hot summer and I learned a new word "roadsideae". This word apparently embraces all flowers and grasses but not butterflies. The letter reported that roadsides near Gourock (with a higher rainfall than here) had magnificent displays of wild flowers. Coming south to Rolvenden Layne, stretches of purple loosestrife are nearing their end, through continuous hot sun, but leafy hawkweed, yellow rattle and grasses are still green and flourishing. We easily forget that many roadsides are bordering ditches and have their roots in moisture. Many readers will have noticed in the hedges blackberries galore but green and small; if rain and sun return, it could be blackberry and apple pie ad infinitum. You may well see in your garden a camberwell beauty, a purple emperor or a clouded yellow butterfly, all normally Continental but reportedly blown across the Channel by the hot weather. I suspect that the most likely is the clouded yellow, which "exploded" onto our southern shores in the hot summer of 1947. I still have a vivid memory of a field near Barton-on-sea golf course, literally covered with this lovely butterfly.

The garden remains a problem. Watering only by can, we are concentrating on keeping alive first year bushes and a few others susceptible to drought, like our small rhododendron and hydrangeas. All our roses are packed round with manure, compost and grass mowings and go on flowering wonderfully. With these hot dry summers it would seem wise to practise this treatment far more widely, especially herbaceous areas. Water is a very precious commodity that the majority take for granted. Today's paper reports an angry reaction from a young woman in Bradford to the installation of stand-pipes. "I am not going to live out of a bucket," she declares, but forgets that thousands of Allied servicemen in the Western Desert lived out of such containers, or less, for weeks so that she could utter those words in 1995.

The other precious commodity is quiet, even silence. I suddenly found it last Sunday. In between officiating at two rather close-timed Communion services, I breakfasted by Bewl Water. The only sounds were the water lapping, some coots calling and an occasional honking from some Canada geese. Otherwise, it was peace and quiet, and quite uplifting.

Early August does not show gardens at their best. Most hybrid and floribunda roses are pausing for breath and recharging batteries and the main herbaceous flowers are over. Many gardeners rely on their annuals and cosseted geraniums and pansies to give colour, with a little help from the watering-can. The nasturtiums along the outside of my road fence are beginning to fade, having given gorgeous colours for two months. Along the same stretch I had planned godetias to follow the flowering pattern but only two plants have appeared, out of 100 seeds! Next year, I must start them in seed compost. The grass is scarcely growing on our lawns, so I followed my usual practice in a dry mid-summer of mowing without the box; a sprinkling of mulch may help the grass to survive alongside the widespread clover.

The good news in the garden comes from the sweet peas. One tripod of exhibition plants are flowering well enough, after 6 weeks, to give me a lovely bowl in the middle of the diningroom table. Also full of flower and scent is my buddleia. In the full midday sun, there is endless movement from bees and butterflies. Yesterday, peacocks and red admirals were in the majority, with a few meadow browns and whites and one tortoiseshell and comma. Perhaps the painted ladies are needing even warmer weather, as in their native North Africa.

On the bird front, an unusual bird has visited a Goudhurst reader. The size of a jackdaw, it is described as black, with a brown ruff, a large beak and inclined to waddle. On a recent visit, the bird had a sparring match with a magpie over the dog's tennis ball and in the end the magpie picked up the ball and flew off with it! Quite a feat. Most garden birds drift further afield at this time of year, but my house martins appear to be teaching their second brood to fly, a lovely sight against a clear evening sky.

Over breakfast a few days ago I saw in my Daily Telegraph the headline "Heatwave stings giant euro wasps into action". Intriguing. Where was this heatwave? It must be referring to the South of France, not England. Heatwave, to me, means at least a

week of very warm weather. So I read on and learned that the journalist had in mind just two warm days the week-end before last and the area affected was East Anglia. Gardeners had been finding the football-like nests of the euro or media wasp, usually hanging in bushes or small trees. A few years ago, several of these nests turned up in Rolvenden, one of them opposite the church. They need to be left well alone or expertly dealt with, if a danger to passers-by. I am reminded that I and others have seen the common wasp earlier than usual; one friend had six in his diningroom two weeks ago. Usually their presence coincides with plums and jam-making, "late summer" in text-book parlance.

Nevertheless, life has not been easy for the insect world. The erratic "stop-go" weather - wet and windy or briefly sunny - inhibits both breeding and activity. For instance, I saw no may bugs in May or June; other friends in different areas have each seen only one. I missed them; their crashing into lighted windows is an integral part of warm mid-summer evenings. Or again, there has been a dearth of the usual night-flying moths and the usual butterflies. Meadow browns and whites are persevering, but fewer than usual. I have seen the occasional speckled wood along a shady footpath and I had a gatekeeper in the garden yesterday. My mauve buddleia is now fully in flower and already I have a crowd of peacocks and red admirals, one or two tortoiseshells but no painted ladies or commas. I have only seen one common blue this season. In a reasonable summer, this delicate butterfly has two broods and is on the wing from May to September. However, the temperature is slowly climbing, as I write, so perhaps August will bring us and the insect world, and the cricketers, some glorious heat.

Deadheading in the garden a few days ago, I suddenly saw fresh droppings on my hollyhocks. Looking up, I saw under the eaves a fresh nest, built recently and at speed. House martins can stay till October, so there is still plenty of time for a lateish brood. Others are already lining up on the wires, plus two swallows. My garden is slowly regaining its colour of June and early July, mainly through its roses. When the latter were re-charging their batteries, two things kept the flag flying. Two self-seeded nasturtiums outside the fence were exuberant with colour, though facing north and in barely an inch of soil. The other exception was my Danse de Feu climber. Whilst the other roses were in low gear, this climber has been in overdrive. The other day I counted over 75 scarlet clusters.

This past fortnight has been rather like the South of France. Daily sunshine and warm evenings have speeded hay-making and combining and allowed relaxed barbecues on patios. Insects also love these conditions and my buddleia is a mass of movement in the sunshine, a delight to the eye - bees competing with numerous, restless butterflies for the nectar. As I hoped, commas come and go, as well as the usual red admirals, peacocks and tortoiseshells. A Sandhurst friend had, in addition, a hummingbird hawk moth on his buddleia, common in Southern Europe but not so much here; they are one of only a few moths that are on the wing in sunshine or warm evenings, hovering in front of strong-scented herbaceous border plants. Mignonette used to be a favourite of theirs but few people grow it these days.

On the bird front, my impression is of many second broods. In my own and friends' gardens there are house martins, pied wagtails, spotted flycatchers and blackbirds, all feeding young, and, in the churchyard hedge, a song thrush with small fledglings in the nest. This latter was cruelly exposed by the hedgecutter (mechanical ?) last week. July is too early to cut and I believe that the law can impose a fine. Churchwardens, beware!

Doing steward duty last week at the Ellen Terry Theatre at Smallhythe, I enjoyed the usual swallows zooming in and out of the theatre annexe, where they nest. Even better news was that the theatre and environs were favoured by more swallows than normal. Five nests produced families. This is contrary to an impression some observers have, i.e. of fewer swallows and house martins this summer. Nevertheless, there has been quite a gathering on the wires down our lane in the mornings - at least 25 swallows and house martins, old and young. A little surprising in its timing, as it is the traditional late August ritual, but it is always a fascinating and welcome sight. My vigil at the Ellen Terry Theatre included one further surprise. Twice, in moments of near-silence, came the soft purring of a turtle dove, that shy summer visitor which is seldom seen.

SEPTEMBER

It is not often that a bird's nest is served up with one's coffee. But, there it was, a linnet's nest complete with five eggs on the tray beside my cup. My friend, Gordon, knew my enthusiasms and I forgot all about the coffee and absorbed the craftsmanship of that nest and its builder. Its framework of twigs was filled in and lined almost entirely with moss and sheep's wool, "local materials", as per Collins' "Guide to Nests and Eggs". Exquisite, proclaiming stability and comfort. As my friend said "We may think that we know how to build anything from a rocket to a rocking-horse but Nature so often cuts us down to size, if we have eyes to see it; that bird had no hands or tools". Sadly, he had found it abandoned in his privet hedge. Perhaps a magpie or a motorist?

The occasion was the annual sponsored bike ride in aid of Kent Churches. Cheerful cyclists were signing in at Old Romney Church, at the start of their day's tour of Romney Marsh. A few paused to step inside that highly interesting unrestored church, with its complete set of 18th century fittings; the whole had just been re-decorated for the first time since Ranks filmed "Dr. Syn" there in the 1960s. Thank goodness, conditions for the cyclists were quite good - sunny, blue sky and slight breeze. They also encouraged me to do a gentle tour.

A great flock of at least 200 lapwings rose up from plough near Ivychurch, but mainly it was pasture, slowly greening, and most sheep still being fed. My way took me past pub and church at St. Mary's, the former associated with Noel Coward and his writings and the latter with the much-loved children's author, Edith Nesbitt. Her memorial inside is well placed beside the font and the simple head-board on her grave testifies to the toughness and longevity of oak. A mile towards Newchurch I stopped the car and paid tribute at the roadside grave of Pilot Officer Arthur Clarke, aged 20, one of "The Few." It was almost to the day that he had been killed in action near that spot 55 years ago in the Battle of Britain. Memorabilia on that grave further stirred the emotions. Some fresh red roses, several British Legion crosses and poppies, and a group photo of some of those carefree pilots of 504 Squadron. Beneath the photo, some homespun verse challenged -

> "Think on me as you pass by,
> Reflect on why I had to die ...
> We surrendered our future
> So you could have yours"

As I stood there, a light aircraft passed directly overhead. Did he learn to fly in exactly that type of plane, I wondered. I also wondered if any of those cyclists paused, just for a moment.

A wedding, a funeral, and now my diary records a baptism, in St. John the Baptist, Harrietsham, still standing in a rural setting, in spite of the proximity of the rushing Channel traffic. It could scarcely have been a happier occasion. The baby was appropriately named Harriet and the sacrament administered by me in a font at which my father and grandfather (both past curates in the parish) must have baptised many other babies earlier this century. Moreover, the font is regarded as one of the finest Norman fonts in Kent. Very small and vocal friends of Harriet had a ring-side view and, not far away, were two very senior and faithful church members, the Misses Cutbush, who remembered my parents. The old and the young - all of us "called to be saints".

Tractors have almost ceased roaring by my house, the cereal harvest is virtually over and hop-picking is in full swing, in changing weather. Temperatures are steadily dropping and my gauge has recorded 43 mm, almost 2 inches, in the first week of September. Quite a difference, bearing in mind the 12 mm measured in the whole of August. That hot, sunny, dry spell of 2-3 weeks seemed to drive away all my garden birds, except, of course, my house martins under the eaves, ever busy and athletic. Blackbirds, thrushes, even starlings and sparrows, had all gone in search of moisture and shade, in spite of my water trough. Occasionally, my robin appeared on the fence. Now starlings are again descending in the field and I see some squabbling among my cotoneaster berries. A Sandhurst friend reported a passing flock of about 30 fieldfares and redwings in their garden on August 28th; quite early, compared with their normal arrival time in October.

Swallows and house martins are lining up. Reports on numbers vary a lot. Large "mixed" gatherings on the wires have been seen in Brookland, Newenden and Rolvenden. Some report no swallows this year in outbuildings but Beckley church had its usual two or three families.

Gardeners are glumly preparing for Autumn Shows these coming Saturdays. On the flower front, not growing dahlias or chrysanthemums I am putting my hopes in Class 31 "Rose; hybrid tea, one bloom" and perhaps in Class 33 "Any flower not listed above"! I also have a resolution for next summer, to copy a neighbour; she has, still flowering, a lovely bed of intermingling godetias and eschscholzias.

I have seen my first "conker" and shared in my first Harvest Festival. I knew then that Autumn had arrived. The "conker" had burst out of its prickly case from a very familiar horse-chestnut. I daily walk Brock under it, so have enjoyed the usual cycle of its stately white "candles", changing to its tiny green fruit and slowly expanding through the summer. All over the country small boys will be throwing up missiles to bring down these cases and their mahogany brown contents. Long may these simple country games continue.

Autumn may be with us but not yet visually. There is scarcely any sign of change of colour. Foliage is generally green and holding. Barely a dozen leaves have yellowed and fallen from my elm. My small rowan, however, has only two scarlet berries left; hardly had they turned from orange, then they were immediately attacked by thrushes, blackbirds and starlings. Greed seems to overcome logic. Yet the cotoneaster tree next-door still carries its berries, presumably because they have yet to turn red. My honeysuckle fruit has turned and, drawing back the curtains this morning, I found a blackbird busily devouring the remainder and quite undeterred by my appearance a few inches away.

September inclines one to review the summer. There seems to have been fewer wasps around and also honey and bumble bees and we can all give several reasons. A few dragon-flies have zoomed around me on the few recent sunny days, when walking on the Levels, but nothing like so many or so often. My buddleia flowering early and briefly meant far fewer red admirals, peacocks and tortoiseshells. Unexpectedly, night-flying moths have greeted me at the windows after dark for several evenings and one medium brown moth near the taps watched me bath last night. Typical, really, of July and August. Like most gardeners, I occasionally disturb from shrubs and plants those lovely tiny orange-brown moths, perhaps a pug or fanfoot. On the credit side, though, a neighbour counted 189 pipistrelle bats in June, based in her loft; we all await with interest the results of this survey by the Bat Society.

The Harvest Festival in Snave was rather moving and romantic. This redundant Marsh church came to life with its annual service of Thanksgiving. Local people and lovers of the Marsh filled the church and were led through Prayer-Book Evensong by three clergy and the Brookland Singers. A few candles, here and there, broke the dim afternoon light, the brown spikes of bulrushes gave a local touch to several floral decorations and on the altar lay a loaf, with two more candles illuminating an open, ancient Bible. From it were read those wise words in Deuteronomy-

"Thou shalt take of the first of all the fruit of the earth which thou shalt bring of thy land that the Lord thy God giveth thee..."

L ast week I indulged in a gentle survey of our local hedgerows. The object was to find material for a floral arrangement, entitled simply "Autumn flowers and foliage" in our village Show. I have never forgotten advice, freely and repeatedly given to all and sundry, by Dorothy Mowll, the queen-bee of floral decoration in Canterbury Cathedral in the early 1950s. In those days Constance Spry had not quite got the grip on floral art as she later achieved. Dorothy stoutly maintained that she normally bought only a few very good blooms and then supplemented them from natural growth of the countryside. "For nine months of the year," she used to say "it is unnecessary to spend large sums of money on exotic flowers and expensive greenery".

The hedgerows and banks did not let me down. There was an abundance of variety and colour. Bracken of all shades from green to brown, willow-herb gone to seed, hemlock likewise, coils of bryony festooned with red berries (often rivalled by rose hips), all these and more were easily available. Not so common this year was old man's beard. Add a few orange-red dahlias for focus and a passable arrangement took shape. The cost, a minimal quantity of petrol and one hour of time.

Heavy mist greeted many of us last Sunday morning. Most beautiful cobwebs also greeted the early riser. The activity of many, many garden spiders glistened on all sides, fairylike, delicate and lovely. Within a few yards I counted twenty creations on buddleia, garden shed and both car mirrors. One just had to pause and enjoy their beauty. Such thoughts slipped easily into others offered at early Communion in Beckley church. Flowers on all sides from their Festival spoke eloquently of other beauty in God's Creation. It was the Sunday, too, when we were bidden to give thanks for "The Few" in the Battle of Britain. What would have happened to our nation and the course of World War II if those young men (some, my friends) had not so courageously fought that battle? We in Kent all seemed to be specially and emotionally involved, from the highest to the lowest. The Home Guard particularly reckoned they were in the front line. Richard Church, well-known Kent author, shared in vigils from Goudhurst's church tower. Vita Sackville-West spent afternoons filling old wine bottles with petrol, paraffin and tar, and then bound two Guy Fawkes squibs round the sides, for the creation of yet more Molotov cocktails. As she wrote in her "Country Notes in Wartime"-

"Every evening at dusk, the tramp of feet goes up my tower, passing the door as I sit working. Very slow and heavy they go, like the tramp of men-at-arms...later I see two figures outlined against the moon behind the parapet...the baker's boy and the blacksmith's son are carrying on the tradition..."

The recent "end of summer" days have been pleasing. Tea or early supper in the garden have been possible. Butterflies have re-appeared. peacocks, tortoise-shells, red admirals and whites have been sampling the few flowers left on my buddleia. It was good, too, to see a large hatch of tortoiseshells in early August, landing on anything that had scent or warmth, and then the period of heavy bouts of rain drove them all into hiding in hedges and sheds and undergrowth. What rain, too! 5 inches in my gauge in August, compared with two inches in 1996.

Gardens looked really battered. Many annuals, flowering well till then, seemed to give up, as did my ageratum, godetia and nasturtiums, but petunias and geraniums soldiered on and are now the main suppliers of colour, helped by a few clumps of antir-rhinums and Michaelmas daisies. Astute readers will at once say "What about dahlias?" and I have to confess that I have none. A bad omission. Dahlias can cheer us all with their warm, glowing colours until the frosts come and we know that winter is near. As usual, my friend, John, has his long, eye-catching row by the main road opposite the Harrier in Sandhurst. Soon, too, will come the annual decision as to when to remove summer bedding and replace with spring plants. Adam Pasco in the Weekend Telegraph gave it as one of his weekend jobs, rather to my dismay. I hang on to any piece of summer colouring as long as possible, even though it means some of the wallflowers do not root strongly enough to withstand winter's onslaught.

Returning for a moment to those lovely warm sunny days in July and August, readers may have noticed one absentee among the butterflies and a preponderance of another. The lovely painted lady was extremely scarce in most parts of Kent, as opposed to last year, when its numbers were well above average. I only saw one on my buddleia this summer. It can be very numerous in its native North Africa and is, therefore, often forced to emigrate to this country and others, for the sake of future generations. On the other hand, the whites have been overwhelming in numbers - all three varieties, the large, small and green-veined, in meadows, gardens and cabbage fields. Although some are native, I expect many of the large whites were migrants from the Continent. One day a Tenterden resident was intrigued to see from his win-dow half a dozen or more whites deliberately flying round and through the water from his sprinkler on the lawn; finally, they settled on the grass and for some seconds indulged in a proper shower.

As for the rest of the news - hop-picking has begun and, with it, the usual nip in the air at 7 am; horse-chestnuts are foremost among the trees in beginning to "turn", and 50 or so house martins (and a few swallows) are daily gathering on the wires down our lane. I watch with some anxiety one of my own house martin families still feeding young on the nest. Africa south of the Sahara is a long way away.

The experts had warned us that strange, exciting things might happen in the entomological world this very hot summer. It is good, therefore, to record that a few did happen in the Weald. Mid-September a Marden family reported that a death's head hawk moth had hatched out in their house. What excitement and what a privilege! As so often, the story began with a caterpillar on the potato tops of a cottage garden in Hunton. Passed to friends in the neighbouring village, it burrowed into the soil mixture of a flower-pot within 24 hours of its discovery, finally to emerge six weeks later. Sadly this magnificent and rare moth would not have survived in our late Autumn climate and conditions. A few death's heads have been recorded this hot summer in the UK generally.

Another unusual migrant, happier in Southern Europe, is the convolvulus hawk moth. One dead specimen was brought in, late September, when they are likely to be on the wing. Found flapping at the roadside, it was first mistaken for a sparrow, indicating its considerable size and wingspan. Another convolvulus was captured in the Linton area, and passed safely to the same Marden family, who released it. Unlike the death's head, it might survive. Quite a few have been seen this summer in the Southern Counties. Clouded yellow butterflies were forecast but few appeared in Kent coastal areas. Nevertheless, our buddleia attracted some really perfect and lovely specimens of commas (the 2nd brood) in September. This very recent warm sunny spell brought a perfect red admiral today to our garage wall and others have been imbibing the nectar of flowers and over-ripe pears and plums to the extent of semi-drunkenness.

In the meantime, the "Fall" is limited in the Weald. A few horse chestnut leaves are turning and some cherries have become a glowing pinky-red and started to fall. Acorns have been showering down upon pavements and grass like confetti. This morning a low-lying mist transformed innumerable cobwebs on the trees and hedges into some Breton lace-making exhibition.

OCTOBER

It is St. Michael and All Angels Day, September 29th, and for me a day when religion and the countryside are inextricably interwoven. I am reminded of letters I used to have in one country parish addressed to "the Vicar of St. Michael the Archangel, the Vicarage..." At once, I felt elevated, almost the Vicar-General of Rome! But, of course, it reminded one of the striking, metaphorical passage in St. John's "Revelation" - "Michael and his angels fought against the dragon and his angels and (the latter) prevailed not..." Churchgoer or not, many of us instinctively refer to our "guardian angel". But real country people still remember the old tradition that "on Michaelmas Day the Devil puts his feet on blackberries", a survival from that biblical battle? No more blackberry picking, therefore, but tidying the garden, making tomato chutney and trying to gauge market prices for selling this year's lambs.

On the bird front, there are gradual changes. My house martins have finally gone and I miss them circling the skies early morning and evening, as one misses faithful friends. Checking on them, early evening, last week-end, I saw unusual movement on my roof-line; to my pleasure, three pied wagtails were there, tails bobbing and making the occasional dart after an insect; moreover, four more were occupying the top of my neighbour's roof. Surely, a family exploring? Where was their nest? A cavity or ledge not too far away, perhaps near the farmyard in Wassall Lane? My faithful robin remains; yesterday his warbling soon stood out, even at midday.

On Saturday the village cricket team played their last game of the season. Always a little sad. The first game often gains a write-up but not the last. Nowhere could I find such a mention in the well-known writings of Edmund Blunden, Robertson-Glasgow or E.V. Lucas, all lovers of the village green. The light was poor, even at 4.30 pm and Rolvenden were batting to Goudhurst's total of 97. Two left-handers facing two slowish bowlers went along steadily before a wicket fell. Then a change of bowling and leg-breaks! But the first over was a disaster - a wide and two longhops, often permitted for leg-breakers. The home batsmen continued unruffled and the match finished with a well-timed square cut to the road boundary and four byes, courtesy the Goudhurst wicket-keeper. Rolvenden had won. The stumps were reluctantly drawn, two players sat down and talked in front of the pavilion, another circled the boundary collecting the flags and a very small boy carried on looking for conkers.

"A ploughman on his legs is higher than a king on his knees". This old saying may be dated but not, I hope, over a prayerful monarch! Nevertheless, it stresses the value of the ploughman. He is still needed on the farm. Indeed his skill is still needed, so Ploughing Matches continue to encourage and set standards, as the Weald of Kent Association did so admirably last Saturday at Reed Court, near Marden.

It seemed, and was, larger than ever - 82 trade stands, 81 ploughmen and more through the gate, north-east wind not withstanding. Barbours, sweaters, wellies and hot coffee were all required rather than ice-creams from the Wimpy's mobile. I tried hard to recall the old County Show at Mote Park in those post-war years (a true agricultural Show) and wondered if it ever embraced 82 stands. Chairman, Mark Scott, hoped the Ploughing Match would remain a genuine farming affair and farmers and country folk in the Weald might even prefer it to the County Show. "It is an enormous asset" he added, "to have one host, Mr. & Mrs. Peter Tipples."

Earlier, as I arrived, I had driven through the area of the ploughing, a salutary reminder, to all who came, of the object of the exercise. Soon, a further credit. The car park was sited in the next field to the stands and the ring; even people on two sticks could walk from one to the other without too much effort. Walking slowly round, I was glad to see livestock represented as well as machinery, fertilisers, country wear and Hubble & Freeman (the supplier of my cricket bats years ago). Here and there were samples of Sussex and Dexter cattle, Charolais sheep and a pen of beautifully turned-out Romneys, a pleasure and a relief in these days of cross-breeding. There was also a brave effort by Sutton Valence Post Office, proclaiming that they sold much more than stamps! Nearby, the Secretary's tent included, beside a busy secretary, an impressive array of cups, a display of hop samples and three exhibitions by Primary Schools on the theme "Food & Farming", won by Hunton C of E Primary; the exhibit was memorable for its scarecrow and harvest loaf, large enough for twenty mice.

Outside was the ring and the Bolebrook Beagles, an uplifting sight as they circled twice. Finally, the stragglers were gathered in by assistant huntsmen and they fraternised in the middle with young and not so young members of the public. Terrier racing was next on the programme, but delayed. A vital piece of equipment was missing. This did not please the terriers. At my feet a brown rough-haired Jack Russell was shouting abuse at a rather smart tan and white cousin a few yards away!

My robin has taken up residence and territory for the winter. It is also a sign, of course, that Autumn is in the process of unfolding its incomparable shades of colours in our daily round. A few days ago I cut the lawn and within 24 hours it was lightly bespattered with leaves, mainly from the elm and virginia creeper. Down the road, a horse chestnut and a cherry are proclaiming "the fall" much more emphatically, and nothing can be more warming to the artistic eye than a cherry on the turn. Moreover, as I cut the lawn, I caught sight of one tiny flower on my winter-flowering yellow jasmine. It was unexpected and exciting; the textbooks give November as the start of flowering.

A few days later, tidying up round the front, I was amused to see no less than six daddy longlegs gently resting on the front door rather like "firstnighters", waiting for the show to start at a London theatre. Their numbers within the house seem to have been greater than usual. I wonder if gardeners have suffered more than usual from their larvae, the leatherjackets, over last year? Earwigs are certainly omnipresent in the house this autumn; one can hardly lift anything without one scuttling away out of the light.

My dog walk the other day ended in an exciting moment. Preparing to enter the car, I was suddenly aware of a large and lovely moth about to come to rest on me. To my surprise, it was a red underwing, the first I had seen for some years although resident mainly in the South and East of England. Near me was a long row of willows which are favoured by both caterpillar and moth.

My tale would not be complete without Harvest Thanksgiving. I was so glad, therefore, to be involved in the celebrations of two parish churches. The second was at East Guldeford, the last piece of Romney Marsh to be reclaimed from the sea, a barn-like church, with a lamb and crook weathervane. Everything else seemed right. A cottage loaf and grapes on the altar. The local and well-known Marsh farmers and their families present and, by the main door, a fleece, symbolic of the wealth and faith that had built those outstanding Marsh churches so many years ago.

Professional writers, particularly journalists, seem to be allowed to conjure up an article out of nothing. One, who shall be nameless, produced a 1,000 word article in a week-end paper, about his border collie who had become a sheep-worrier. To any experienced dog-owner, this was "old hat" and did not deserve a fee of several hundred pounds. Nor did it require forced face to face encounters with a local farmer's ram. As a lifelong countryman I have always seen it as my first duty to discipline a dog not to chase sheep or any other valuable livestock. There are, roughly speaking, two methods - by immediate punishment or by canine example. The second is the easier. Our first Jack Russell, Chippy, had to learn by punishment and in later years I have seen him chasing a hare across Romney Marsh straight through a flock of sheep without deviating one foot. My present Jack Russell, Brock, learned by example. Walking with the two farm dogs on my daughter's farm as a puppy, he immediately learned the basic lesson. One did not chase sheep or chickens. They are part of "the establishment". The occasional pheasant, maybe, was fair game and most definitely any rabbit having a siesta or a nibble within 100 yards of a terrier's orbit. They must be removed at once. Perhaps Jack Russells are in certain ways more intelligent than border collies?!

The Autumn is slowly gathering momentum. With the recent short burst of rain alternating with warm sunny periods, the leaves that have turned are beginning to fall. Frogs Lane, near me, is lined on both sides with a pleasing yellow-brown border, hiding both ruts and rubbish. As usual, leaves from cherry, horse-chestnut and beech are leading the "fall". Up my road, though, is an exception to the autumn process. A stretch of ivy has blossomed (always later than other plants) and its green and gold flowers are attracting bees, wasps and flies in the sunshine. These warm sunny days have also encouraged the dragon-flies to continue flying. Yesterday, down a farm track with Brock, I stood enthralled as I watched those lovely insects hunting a newly sown field and into the woodland beside it. I felt sad that the adult life-span is about a month.

My Shell Nature Book, published years ago in 1964, remains a very relevant pictorial guide to flowers, trees, birds and mammals and wild-life generally through the year. The initial section "Flowers of the Countryside" is illustrated beautifully by Edith and Rowland Hilder. Moving into the next section, "Trees and Shrubs", I paused at October. The script begins "This is the elderberry month... purple black-berries, sagging from each low elder bush..." Is this true this year? Or is it that many have not yet changed colour and therefore not caught the eye? October is certainly the month for other berries and nuts. "Conkers" have been falling for several weeks, acorns are turning brown on several neighbouring oak trees and hazel nuts should be ripe. S. R. Badmin's water-colour of foliage in October did, however, strike a different note from our prevailing landscape; all the beeches, chestnuts and cherries had turned an overall gold, only the oaks, traditionally late, remained green. We are at present still in summer garb.

October begins to nudge some wild-life into hibernation or departure to warmer climates. The drop in temperature on the 3rd, the day of the Ploughing Match, found a good many swallows and house martins already on their way south. Indoors, daddy-longlegs disappeared from the windows at once, only to reappear in reduced numbers a week later. Some warm sunny afternoons then enticed several wasps into the house, looking for sugar, and numerous dragon-flies on the Rother Levels, just enjoying the sun on their backs. Earwigs are always with us and mate in the autumn; they are alleged to guard and care for their 20-80 eggs under a stone or in some hollow all through the winter. Their ability to hide in the smallest space is incredible. Two evenings ago, I assisted one out of the hand-basin onto the floor and quickly lost him; the very next morning, using the toilet roll, I found him asleep or hiding under two thicknesses of paper.

My diary records other miscellany. A hedge-sparrow with a white head frequents a neighbour's garden. My smallish sweet william plants have only survived through regular protection by Slug-death - a nightly battle. Over two inches of rain fell in Rolvenden Layne in the first fortnight of the month. Local Canada geese have been noisy and a flight of ten over the house cheered my breakfast last Monday. Ditto my Sunday breakfast after the majestic sight of two mute swans crossing my vision as I drove across Hexden Channel.

Next Sunday is also St. Luke's Day, a day of thanksgiving for all medical knowledge and of prayer for all doctors and nurses. How very fortunate we are. One cannot begin to calculate what a difference the memory and the pen of St. Luke has made to the world. Those incomparable parables. "Who is my neighbour?" "A certain man went down from Jerusalem to Jericho..."

This morning we all woke up to find signs of the first real frost of the winter. Somehow it seemed to complete the whole range of weather conditions that we have experienced this past fortnight. Gale force winds with bursts of heavy rain brought some leaves and masses of the heavy acorn crop down onto the ground and my rain gauge measured 3 inches in the first half of October. Yet we have also enjoyed warm sunny afternoons and temperatures in the early 70s. As a result, there is already striking autumnal foliage; beech leaves are now competing with cherry and chestnut, which are dropping widely. Maybe duffle coats need to be shaken and prepared for use -

> When chestnut leaves do fall,
> Cotton ain't no good at all.

Understandably, bird movement is uncertain and patchy. Single swallows have been sighted in Romney Marsh and near the Swale Estuary in North Kent over the past seven days, as well as a house martin. A few redwings have arrived near the Swale for the winter and a flock of lapwings was seen in the same area, perhaps down from the North of England. My lament about lapwing scarcity, in this column three weeks ago, was fully substantiated in the last week-end Telegraph, who gave a full page coverage to comment by Mr. Robin Page on reports and surveys of the lapwing population. Its decline of 50% in just 20 years appears to be due to modern farming methods (as I suggested) and an increase of predators (crows, magpies and foxes) which are not being controlled. It was heartening to read of two farmers in East Anglia who had highly productive farms and yet were creating conditions for lapwings and controlling predators. Members of the RSPB might like to protest at the Society's recent report "Birds in the Balance" not including the lapwing in the 23 species listed. Last week I read with sadness a glowing tribute among the obituaries to Mr. Stuart

Ogg at the ripe age of 92. Many will not have heard of him but he deserves a salute from all of us who garden. As the writer began "He was one of the great flower show-men of the 1950s and 1960s." Nowadays it is relatively easy for a good gardener who can talk knowledgeably and persuasively on television to become a household name. Stuart Ogg was in a different class to such people altogether. He was a real and skil-ful grower, particularly of dahlias, chrysanthemums and, above all, delphiniums. He made his name entirely by results and by lecturing. Over 40 years, he rarely failed to win the top honours and, as one who heard him, I can vouch for his lectures being quite memorable.

Winter seems to have come, and rather suddenly at that. Four frosts in as many days have covered the Rolvenden area. My duffle coat has been in use the last three early morning dog walks. The clocks have changed and we are facing a week-end of Hallow E'en, All Saints' day and All Souls' day, as well as bonfires and fireworks in honour of Guy Fawkes. All point towards winter and dark evenings and log fires.

Nevertheless, country folk used to celebrate all these days wholeheartedly. Ceremonial fires lit, church bells rung and souling customs carried out -

> Remember the departed for holy Mary's sake,
> And of your charity, pray gi'us a big soul-cake.

Survivals in the 1990s are, I suppose, Hallow E'en dances, illuminated by "pumpkins" and rather moving candle-lit services in some parish churches on All Soul's day. Guy Fawkes celebrations continue as ever, perhaps more expensively. May I plead with dog and cat owners to have special care of their pets this seven day period? May I remind housewives also that pumpkins make excellent soup?

NOVEMBER

I believe that I am living with a miracle and that miracle is lying, stretched out on the rug beside me. It is Brock, my Jack Russell. Exactly two weeks ago, he was run over by a van. It was horrific to see and two other witnesses were quite sure that he had been killed. Nevertheless, he fought for life in the face of deep shock and a broken pelvis and hind leg and has survived, with the expert help of modern veterinary practice. I still can hardly believe it. I need scarcely add that nursing a badly injured dog on one's own is an enormous emotional strain. For the first few days at home, Brock could hardly move or stand. I had to guess his thoughts and requirements all through the day and carry him most places. Strain though it has been, I was so very glad to dedicate myself to him. He had been a lifeline since Angela died and he now desperately needed me. Our bonding is doubly strong.

Some of you who read the Daily Telegraph may have noted a furore over common ivy. It all began with an article in the Week-end Telegraph describing ivy as "a serial strangler on the loose in the countryside"! The writer went on to claim that it threatens to "exterminate 75% of our native trees"; also that ivy's dominance in the country scene was relatively modern, as can be seen when comparing Constable's landscapes with those of current artists; let ivy go back to where it belongs - walls, old barns, ruins and churches! The writer has clearly not heard of Quinquennial Inspections by professional architects who pounce on the slightest external growth on churches.

As this was published a week before National Tree Week, beginning November 20th, it called for attention and thought. Were these claims really true? I began by consulting my quick but sound reference book, the AA Book of the Countryside and I read "Ivy uses tree trunks solely for support. Its climbing roots draw no nourishment through the tree bark nor does it strangle the tree..." Then I strolled slowly round

Rolvenden Layne, deliberately noting the state of all mature trees, including those in hedgerows. Only one third had ivy on the trunks and most of those were to be found in a small copse that had not had even minimal management for 20 years or more. In due course, letters appeared in the Daily Telegraph in praise of ivy, pointing out the original error and the positive aspects - nesting niches for certain birds, food for some insects and the copious flow of nectar from its flowers late into the Autumn, extolled in this column only last month. The lovely delicate holly blue, both caterpillar and butterfly, are specially drawn to ivy. So, all in all, I suspect that there is not quite the crisis suggested by Mr. Richardson in the Telegraph. Let us all continue to plant trees and treat ivy with understanding and tolerance. We can then sing "the Holly and the Ivy" at Christmas with reasonable sincerity.

Winter is slowly gathering momentum. Leaves are falling in increasing numbers, wallflowers have replaced antirrhinums, godetia and ageratum in my garden and the geraniums have given up and must be potted and brought in. With winds being more frequent and stronger, I must reduce the height of some roses to avoid loosening of the roots. At the same time, I am hoping that St. Martin's little summer will induce some rose-buds to open up and flower. As a portent of things to come, I was shown, two weeks ago, some shy yellow primroses in a neighbour's garden - "a well-known Spring flower" says my Oxford Book of Wildflowers.

On the bird front, there are still confused signs. Five swallows were seen briefly over an Appledore garden on November 3rd. Fieldfares and redwings have arrived in the same area and in North Kent and, as mentioned last week, widgeon and white-fronted geese on Sheppey and Romney Marsh. Mute swans are gathering in small groups for the winter on the dykes and fields of the Rother Levels but the Bewicks have allegedly not arrived yet from Northern Europe on the Marsh itself.

It is also the week leading up to Remembrance Sunday and memories come thick and fast to those of us alive in the Second World War - incidents and people, sacrifices, feats of endurance and courage, loyalty and discipline. Many who dug for victory by day were Home Guards by night, watching and waiting. I am reminded of my own small section on Cleeve Hill (about 1200 ft) overlooking Cheltenham and Evesham. A little above us, a broad plateau on which "parachutists might land in large numbers" according to our ex-Indian Army colonel! So we oiled and polished our one Lewis machine-gun, off a First World War aeroplane, a little more vigorously and gazed out across hills and valleys, a typical Cotswold countryside.

Currently, though, I have been selling poppies, reminding all of us of those open, rather drab fields of Flanders and their red flowers. Perhaps we need stronger reminders of those thousands who lie there in neat rows and their undoubted message to all of us, especially the young. We can read it on Tenterden's War Memorial -

Live thou for England, We for England died.

One of my nut containers has disappeared. Yesterday it was swinging from the lowest branch of my elm, with a tit or starling feeding. Today it has gone, with the looped string still hanging from the tree and no sign of it anywhere within yards. I darkly suspect a magpie that occasionally hangs about in the elm, surveying activities in the garden. They are born hoarders and thieves and the shiny metal-work may have excited it.

More and more leaves are falling. I paused on my afternoon dog walk to enjoy at my feet a lovely round carpet of maple leaves, shades of red blending with rich gold, a mosaic of delight to the eye. My elm leaves, less striking, are beginning to cover some herbaceous plants and a corner of the lawn. But what matter? A little untidiness is bearable for a while and an unconscious relief from orderliness and perfection. In any case, C.E. Lucas-Phillips in his "New Small Garden" reminds us that "Nature's own method of feeding her plants is by leaf-fall, and man cannot do better". Or again, Christopher Lloyd extols the smell of Autumn and writes "the smell of decaying leaves is so deliciously bitter-sweet as to affect our emotions strongly..." Finally, blackbirds and thrushes love them and will scratch away happily for hours, to the surprise of earthworms and other insects.

On the bird front, it is good to hear of a few curlew having been seen recently near the Levels. The muddy stubble fields near the A28 Hexden bridge might even attract them there. Their song, loud, slow and liquid, is always exciting. Even more evocative to me is the honking of Canada geese in flight overhead, but only twice have I enjoyed that sound in the past month. Unlike a London street, though, every day in the country brings a change of scenery and sound and can uplift our life that day.

Last Sunday showed the Church in step with this changing scene. It was the Sunday next before Advent and there came those well-known words of the Collect "Stir up, we beseech thee, O Lord, the wills of thy faithful people..." The Church's year was ending and she was asking for action by the faithful. In addition, the Prayer-Book bade us listen to that haunting last chapter of Ecclesiastes "Remember thy Creator in the days of thy youth ... Before the years draw nigh". The end of a year and perhaps the end of some life. Please God, that person was in tune with their Creator at the last.

November tends to be the month for village cricket clubs to hold their AGMs. Your scribe has already been to two and is due for a third shortly. All are different in atmosphere but contain the common factor of relaxed and direct comment, not always with the permission of the chair! I know from personal experience that chairing such a meeting calls for every ounce of expertise and tolerance and guile.

Club A met in their pavilion, in close proximity to the bar, which is perfectly normal but particularly deserved as, in this case, the bar was itemised in the accounts as having made a profit of £1000! What village club could better that? The Chairman kindly delayed the start to allow for the late arrival of two or three players "unavoidably delayed" and then, with 15 present, we were off into the usual AGM Agenda, initially the reports of officers. There emerged a picture of wet weather and cancellations in May followed by the fine dry spell in July, with hard wickets and some victories. Special rosettes were given to two brothers who mainly prepared the wickets and two other stalwarts who were building up a growing youth section. Some boys who began did not know whether they were right or left-handers - and we are talking about a Kent village! Edmund Blunden, the Kent poet, whose childhood "breathed cricket as naturally as air", would have died for shame.

Club B met in the back room of a pub, also typical and convenient. The Chairman, who began on time, claimed that it was the biggest gathering for some years. In contrast to Club A, it included four ladies, who were in fact the treasurer, the scorer and two assistant fundraisers. Their presence was welcome and civilising but did not prevent the meeting being jolly, noisy and spontaneous. Every item was keenly discussed - the results, the weather, subscriptions (not all paid, and names were read out) and the fixtures. Sportsmanship was lacking in at least two opponents, so what should be done? Was it the over-competitive influence of League cricket seeping in to friendly' games? Ground, equipment and AOB were not forgotten but adequately covered before the finish and immediate removal to the roaring fire in the bar.

November is also the time for remembrance' - All Saints Day, All Souls and then Remembrance Sunday, still, thank God, widely observed by all ages in this country. Many claim the Cenotaph to be the most deeply moving of all the ceremonies and yet the utter contrast of a small village remembering its dead and praying for peace can be equally moving. It was my privilege to lead such a service last Sunday high up on the North Downs at Wormshill. Everything was simple and very rural - a timber porch, two clanging bells, a small chamber organ, no choir or sung Glorias but a said Family Communion with a Remembrance theme and numerous family groups. In our prayers for those who died we included Elsie Walters killed by shrapnel on her farm during the Battle of Britain. Unusual and rather moving was the action of eight Sunday School children who formed a circle in the chancel. Having received the Peace from me, they solemnly gave it to each other and then moved into the nave to give it to each of the congregation with much childish spontaneity and fun. What could have been more suitable on that Sunday - the Peace of the Lord working through ordinary people?

Why do some people consign their garden rubbish to the refuse lorry? Or perhaps worse, dump it the other side of the road on the verge or in the hedge? It is, surely, both mistaken and wasteful. If it is unsuitable for the compost heap, it can be put on the bonfire and burnt. Very few gardens in a village are too small for one or the other and can usually accommodate both. Autumnal prunings are sometimes rather long or bulky but, if chopped into 6-12 inch lengths

they provide roughage and aeration for the grass mowings, small weeds and cabbage leaves on the compost, all assisted by some rotting compound. Alternatively, there is the bonfire for tougher rubbish. Few gardens in the Layne are smaller than mine and yet I easily manage a good bonfire on still days without, I hope, incurring the wrath of my neighbours. In Autumn and Spring the bonfire ash, like the compost, can be transferred to the garden and I'm quite sure that compost kept hundreds of plants alive in the drought this summer. In addition, I confess I love a bonfire.

Meanwhile, we have been enjoying the benefits of a ridge of high pressure, so strange things continue to happen in garden and home. One friend was stung by a wasp when having lunch; another picked a bowl of roses for the table yesterday and found several gladioli in flower. In my own garden the antirrhinums still offer patches of pink and red.

But conditions are changing now. Three successive white frosts have destroyed all my nasturtiums, which produced enormous growth in September after the rain. My few dahlias have virtually given up. The leaves of some trees have suddenly started to fall. On the morning of the second frost, I watched fascinated as two nearby ashes shed their leaves continuously and comprehensively rather like those poppies in the Albert Hall as they flutter down upon the motionless Service personnel after the Last Post at that annual Service of Remembrance. The great majority of leaves, though, are still holding and many have not even begun to turn. Quite a change from last year, when my diary entry for November 23rd reads - "The majority of leaves have now fallen, except for a few oaks..."

A few days ago a small tortoiseshell butterfly appeared at my study window but, with more frosts possible, it may already have gone into hibernation in some attic or woodshed or even church. Hedgehogs will also be doing the same, perhaps in some mature herbaceous border or leaf-pile. Young ones from September litters are still around and news reached me of a Cranbrook resident sheltering eight young hedge-hogs in her large greenhouse. At night they all huddle together in a corner. I am at once reminded of wrens who are specially known for their coming together into some sheltered corner of a building on a winter's night. As contrasting behaviour, my winter jasmine has come into flower. Unless frosts are severe, its yellow flowers will continue and give colour to the small arrangement on my desk through to February and sight of Spring!

I find it difficult not to start with the weather. Within a week we have been subjected to the whole range of mood. Last week-end we experienced thunder, lightning, torrential rain, to be succeeded, as I write, by a calm, a widespread over-night frost and blue sky and sunshine.

Sunday produced 1½ inches in my gauge and so violent was the rain at times that stretches of the A268 (Hawkhurst to Newenden) were semi-flooded mid-afternoon and some car engines stopped. Like many, I was earlier part of a large Remembrance parade service in the square at Ticehurst, supported by a smart pipe and drum band. By a miracle we escaped being soaked, a downpour occurring both immediately before and after. An extra and rather moving touch was provided by a Lament by the leading piper after the Last Post and Reveille. Elsewhere, there was standing water in the Rother Valley itself, as well as the Levels and along Hexden Channel, gulls swimming happily near Northiam station. At least two inches seem to have fallen in the three days, Saturday to Monday.

Yet I am told that Bewl Water is less than half full. The leaves having "turned" late, the recent rough weather has now brought them down in quantity and only given visitors to Bewl a brief period of the usual eye-catching colouring. The landscaping and the planting of about 10,000 trees 20 years ago once again reveals the skill and sensitivity of Dame Sylvia Crowe, who died recently. Her memorial there and in other gardens and parks lives on, uplifting the hearts of thousands.

The weather has, of course, battered most flowers in the garden. Colour, other than browns and greens, is at a premium. Nevertheless, I still try and keep a few arrangements going in my house. My Angela (who was so good at floral art) unknowingly taught me a lot and, early in our married life, we heard a memorable lecture by the incomparable Constance Spry. She was such a good speaker that I have never forgotten the guidelines she gave. I believe that every house interior needs one or more floral arrangements, however small, to take away the formality and squareness of furniture and to give it a creative, living touch.

DECEMBER

Yesterday I suddenly saw Father Christmas in full regalia driving a bus. Such was my astonishment that I failed to check in my driving mirror whether it was a supermarket special or a service bus. Surely the Maidstone & District would not encourage such practice? His beard might get tangled up in the steering wheel or in the ticket apparatus. Whatever it was, I knew then that the Christmas festivities had really begun.

But, in a way, Nature had forestalled this general human rejoicing. For weeks now, all female holly trees have been covered with their striking red berries. Their display this year has been widespread and wonderful and heart-warming, quite exceptional. Moreover, they have not been ravaged in the usual way by starlings, thrushes and field-fares, mainly because the fieldfares and redwings have not arrived from Scandinavia. A recent gathering of ornithologists from across the County reported scarcely any fieldfares at all and only a minimum of redwings. The cause is at present a mystery. Have they even arrived in Holland or Northern Germany? They are certainly missing a feast, as there is also a bumper crop of hawthorn berries.

The holly trees may have led the way but GPO came a close second. Late November we were presented with their Christmas issue and the robin, our much loved national bird. If it was not to be a religious theme, then perhaps the robin is the next best. We all love to have at least one in our garden. As if to say 'thank you', the robin is undoubtedly more numerous in many gardens this winter, jaunty yet circumspect, keeping a beady eye on the remains on the bird-table. One friend has at least three in his garden and yesterday he saw two together on his bird-table - no internecine strife but perhaps a truce à la Bosnia? The robin also holds its own on Christmas cards. Today we received a card with no less than four portrayed, each in a typical pose such as you might see from your kitchen window. One is perched on a fork handle and another seems to be emerging from a nest in the axle of an old wooden wheelbarrow.

Nevertheless, in spite of the robin's popularity on Christmas cards, I venture to suggest that the most popular theme this year is that of angels. I say this, having been on weekly duty at the Charity Card shop in Tenterden where there are the cards of 35 national and area charities. Angels seem to predominate and I am delighted. They are God's messengers, unseen and unrecognised by the majority in our technological society. The Bible tells us that they played their part in preparing and announcing to a chosen few the most important birth in the history of the world. May God bless you all this Christmas and may you echo in your hearts the words of the heavenly host -

"Glory to God in the highest, and on earth peace, goodwill toward men"

It is difficult, if not impossible, to separate religion from the countryside. Not only is the latter God's creation but faith arose from nomadic man's instinctive need for a God. In due course, Christ was born in a stable, not even a house, and grew up in a village and talked and taught in terms utterly familiar to country folk. Most of his parables were drawn from the daily rural scene of that period and yet are still easily understood and applicable. Down the ages the feast days and traditions of the Christian Church have been imperceptively woven into the pattern of country people and their lives. I dare to hope that this may continue to be a deeper influence than technology and materialism.

For some days I have not been surprised, therefore, to sense a sort of Advent atmosphere around me. For the second successive day it is grey, overcast and still. Both Nature and farmers might be described as "watching and waiting", as religious folk are exhorted to do in this season leading up to Christmas. They might both be asking "Will it be a hard winter or not?" The hop farmer is not sure when he can proceed with planting his hops or the sheep farmer, when to start feeding his sheep. Many oak and beech leaves are still clinging uncertainly to the trees. In the garden my lilac buds are not so forward as last December and the camellias seem reluctant to show their full hand. Without searching among the piles of leaves I have not yet found any bulbs emerging. On the religious front, it was very good to hear last Sunday in the parish church the ancient words of the Collect in the Prayer-Book -

"Blessed Lord, who has caused all Holy Scriptures to be written for our learning; Grant that we may in such wise hear them, read, mark, learn and inwardly digest them..."

Familiar words to churchgoers for 400 years on Bible Sunday and all part of the "watching and waiting" for Christmas Day. Without the Word of God in that great Book, there would be no knowledge and no faith and no hope. It was, therefore, utterly reassuring and legally right to note that a complete Bible rested, solid and permanent, on the lectern of this country church. Such surely should be the case in every parish church in England?

We were all warned. Mr. Ron Lobeck on the weather last night urged us to "wrap up well" and this morning an angry orange-red sunrise reinforced that warning. By mid-morning the snow had begun to fall and within an hour there was an inch on the ground. Romney Marsh reported three inches and likewise the Tonbridge area. Winter had really come. Trees, hedges, the whole countryside had an ethereal quality about them all. It was a landscape that Rowland Hilder loved and so often painted.

Reactions, of course, varied. British Rail cried "foul" and claimed it was not ready for "this particular type of snow", so crawled at one mph along the branch line to Ashford. Motorists going to work gritted their teeth and reduced speed to 40mph, thus creating queues on motorways. All the starlings in the neighbourhood seemed to descend upon our bird-table and environs, swamping the few sparrows and pushing the gentler, more polite chaffinches and dunnocks to the fringes. The robin bided his time in the herbaceous border and the blue and great tits just carried on with the nuts, safe from bully-boys in our new RSPB feeding "cage". The sheep in the field over the fence also carried on grazing, snow or no snow; they clearly did not care if they now looked in urgent need of a bath. They knew that they were warm and they knew they had to go on feeding until the shepherd brought them those "extras" in the feeding troughs.

Post-lunch I had Brock's reaction. I think it was his first experience of snow and he also looked in need of a bath. Puzzled and excited, he charged in amongst it, racing across the fields alongside the farm track. Later I could see his legs in the air - amazingly, he had found something smelly and brown through that layer of snow. Round a corner we found a hen pheasant scuttling into a sheltering copse and, a little later, two cock pheasants perched sedately on a gate. They dislike snow and, according to gamekeepers, will often spend up to three days in a tree in snowy conditions. Heavy rain they find just as unpleasant and farm gates and low branches are exactly what they need for drying out. Some, of course, seek shelter and food in people's gardens. Two days ago a cock pheasant honoured us with his presence, having first checked us over from the fence. The corn I threw down was a little too close to the house, so he foraged for five minutes before flying up and into the field to inspect the sheep troughs. A friend in the village claims to have had the same pair nesting in her garden for three years; I gather that this is just possible but more likely to be the same hen, with different cocks. Pheasants are to me a very pleasing feature of our countryside. The Romans did a useful job introducing them from Asia, in keeping with their advanced civilised standards. The cock especially is a beautiful bird but, whether cock or hen, they have a quietly dignified air as they stroll across the paddock or up some woodland drive. But for ourselves the best immediate advice could be:-

"When snow and frost are both together
Sit by the fire and spare shoe leather"

The cycle may continue but, within it, "personnel" and habits change. Mammals and birds come nearer human habitation. In my garden, at least two blackbirds move around most of the day; several bluetits have reappeared, sampling the nuts and investigating branches and trunks for insects; in the field, over the fence, large mistle thrushes and occasional fieldfares have joined starlings in probing the thicker grass and the sheep-droppings. Twice a day now, rooks descend, too, in numbers, and even invade my garden at feeding-time if they time it right. Smaller creatures, of course, hibernate.

A gardener told me recently that they seldom tidy their herbaceous border till the Spring, as an offering to hedgehogs and perhaps toads. A neighbour has 80-90 pipistrelle bats in her roof space; she counted them one fine summer evening as they streamed out. Another contact told me of tens of wrens huddling into the corner of a porch at night; and, incidentally, where are all the wrens? I fear their numbers are down. But, thank goodness, we are almost onto St. Thomas' day, 21st of December, and the shortest day. Hooray! But spare a thought for St. Thomas, "the doubting apostle". Liturgically, being so near Christmas Day, he has a raw deal, but not this year. His day falls on a Sunday so, although he has to compete with Advent 4, I'm sure that, in most parish churches, he will have a mention, in the words of his Collect. It is good to see more cribs around in shops and public places than there used to be. One of the best in Tenterden High Street might well be that of my friend Barry's Flower Shop - some well-dressed, tall figures, with imitation bales and the usual extras. A contrast can be seen inside Barclays Bank. The figures appear to be hand-knitted and stuffed; they may lack virility but, instead, suggest the humility of the shepherds and the holy family. Whatever medium or style, they all seek to proclaim the greatest miracle in the history of mankind.

The setting was historical and grand - St. George's Ivychurch in Romney Marsh. The occasion was this year's Carol Service to celebrate the birth of Christ. Ten willing and brave members of the City of Canterbury Brass Band were there to give emphasis and resonance to the well-known music and singing. It was not easy. The church was very cold and the congregation, eclectic. In addition, trombones and trumpets seemed a little strange in a 15th century chancel, which would have been more familiar with strings and woodwind.

Nevertheless, the traditional carols and readings were offered to the Almighty. The Christmas story gradually unfolded, beginning with Isaiah's famous prophesy - "For unto us a child is born.... and the government shall be upon his shoulder..." and concluding with St. John's declaration "In the beginning was the Word". In between, we remembered the inspiration of poets and musicians, and sang heartily, partly to keep warm. Full marks to our brass ensemble for leading us at a spanking pace through "Ding dong merrily on high", which almost had us ringing the bells and running round the aisles.

Soon after, there was indeed a little drama and movement. About 20 children and adults slowly carried lighted christingles in procession round the darkened Early English nave, to finish in a wide circle round the crib in a brief moment of obeisance. It reminded me of a memorable night during Christmas 1962. As a young parish priest I walked over from the Rectory at midnight through driving snow to lock up the church. Entering by the west door, I suddenly realised that the huge church was not dark. On the sanctuary step there was a tiny crib light which, small though it was, transformed the interior. It was moving and symbolic. The light of the baby Child, overcoming the darkness in a snowy, stormy world.

Christmas presents are often surprises. They are doubly so if they come from an unexpected source. Such was my first present. It hung on the handle of my front door and, inside the carrier bag, were no less than three nut containers, with nuts in them. All this, because, two weeks ago, I had revealed the mysterious loss of a container off a tree. What a thoughtful and kind act from an unknown reader, and I do thank them most warmly.

That same week I also received interesting and informative letters from two other readers. One had had a long battle of wits with a particular squirrel which specialised in the theft of nut containers; the householder eventually won, by means of an ingenious sliding cover. The other letter was full of observations, over the seasons, from a boat moving up and down the Rother between Blackwall and Bodiam, ranging from buzzards overhead to rescuing lambs from the river. As a final tit-bit in the "nut war", a Sandhurst friend discovered, after keeping watch, that her culprit was a cock pheasant; it had learned how to fly up and dislodge the container.

Pheasants or squirrels, they are blissfully unaware of Christmas, conscious only of the need for food, whatever the conditions. Thankfully the pace of the countryside and its wildlife remains the same, unaffected by rush in the High Street. Apart from the attractive angelic stamps, my first taste of the real Christmas came last Sunday. Daughter, Penny and I and grandchildren attended the annual Carol Service in St. George's Ivychurch, in the middle of Romney Marsh. The rooks on the Rectory trees looked down upon us quizzingly as we all walked up the church path; they are used to a quiet life - no peals of Grandsire from the church bells, no large crowds.

That afternoon the grand church was alive with activity and sound. In the medieval chancel, the Canterbury City Brass Band was tuning up, in the nave, families were slowly taking their seats, groups of children were dressing up in far corners - shepherds, kings and numerous angels, with suitable angelic faces and lovely crocheted shawls. Church wardens looked anxious, tea-ladies put out more sausage rolls and mince pies and the band gave us an aperitif of Christmas music. Finally, a welcome by the Vicar, the dedication of a new flower pedestal and into the opening carol "O little town of Bethlehem", words that have never failed to stir human hearts. We had come to the heart of the matter, beside which all the Christmas trimmings are temporary and insignificant. Whether at Carol Service or Midnight Mass we come together to proclaim that "Christ was born of Mary" and pray that that "Holy Child of Bethlehem" will "be born in us today".

It was almost St. Thomas' Day, the shortest day of the year and the occasion was the annual Carol Service at St. Mary's, East Guldeford, Sussex. About 70 people of all ages made their slippery way in winter sunshine across the field to this barn-like building, with its twin roofs and bellcote. I wonder how many knew that it stands on one of the last areas of Romney Marsh to be recovered from the sea? Consecrated on September 5th 1505, it has stood, squat and compact, defying the worst of wind and weather for nearly 500 years in that flat but romantic landscape and providing shelter for the faithful few to continue the cycle of worship to Almighty God.

So we all stood in its high box pews and gave thanks once again for the good news of Christmas, led by the Rye Singers. Few things are more moving than when that first verse of "Once in Royal David's city" breaks the silence, today sung beautifully by their conductor, as clear and in tune as any cathedral chorister. So we are led gently into the service as the Singers in their green robes processed up the church and into the sanctuary ..." and our eyes at last shall see Him, through His own redeeming Love". Above the Singers were 30 lighted candles on the reredos and, even higher, were the famous multi-coloured angels, painted above the east window and many carrying musical instruments. "Hail, thou that art highly favoured, the Lord is with thee; blessed art thou among women..." spoke the angel through the mouth of the reader, and the Singers echoed the words with their "Angelus ad virginem". Thus, readings and music carried us slowly and expertly through the Christmas story. Sometimes we relaxed in the traditional tunes, sometimes we were stirred by some negro spiritual or caught up by the catchy rhythm of "Joy shall be theirs in the morning".

By 3.30 pm the sun was disappearing and the light beginning to fade. The tortoiseshell butterfly, fluttering on the east window, had folded its wings in a corner. The 30 mini-candles seemed to be shining more brightly and possibly competing with the Victorian oil lamp burning on the pulpit closeby. All was well though. There was still light enough for a lovely rich contralto solo "Light a candle for Christmas" as well as a violin solo and prayers and a full-throated "Hark! The herald angels sing" from us all. Back then to the road and home, all of us, one hoped, uplifted and renewed in our Faith in the Child Jesus, the Light of the world.

A MISCELLANY

L ast week, a wedding; this week, a funeral, a special funeral. All the village came, from the highest to the lowest. Albert (but John to many, and Effie to others) had become over the years "Mr. Rolvenden". Though not born here, he had been grafted as a boy onto the central stem of village life. In 1940, as a young Private in the Buffs, he achieved a remarkable feat. Taken prisoner at St. Valéry, with others of the 51st Highland Division, he had escaped and walked 1200 miles through France to the Pyrenees, with only two words of French 'oui' and 'non'. He once "borrowed" a bicycle and on another occasion he took a short train trip. Otherwise he relied on his Gallic appearance, his commonsense and his rural resource-fulness; as one official history puts it - "guiding himself by kilometre stones and maps stolen from telephone callboxes". Sadly, this extraordinary bid for freedom did not result in his return home at once, but it did unknowingly produce a rich dividend.

Fifty years had gone by. Family, building work, football and cricket (including two hat-tricks in an innings against Stone!) had kept Albert occupied and happy. Finally, less active, he watched over the village from his chair beneath the shadows of church and chestnut trees at the Wittersham turning. Some waved, some stopped to talk. He knew most people and most people knew him. So the church was packed to pay their last respects. Six young footballers, immaculate in white shirts and ties, carried him in, to the strains of Lili Marlene. An emotional moment. Then the first hymn "Jerusalem" - "And did those feet..." His feet! They carried him across France! How utterly appropriate, but he was, of course, always proud of his country and his war service. So, through the Prayer-Book service and the familiar words "In my Father's house are many mansions..." and a personal tribute from Jim, another Rolvenden "boy", before commendation and "Abide with me". There remained his exit. The same immaculate footballers, steady and slow, carried him out - no organ, just the

strains of "Je regrette rien...". Stirring memories for some. Specially so, perhaps, for a short, white-haired man sitting quietly in the south aisle. He it was, a young Englishman, resident in the Jura foothills, whom Albert had encountered at the end of his long walk. Tremendously impressed by Albert's feat, Tony Brooks had put him in touch with an escape route and then used it himself. Barely six months later, he was parachuted into France and became one of the most successful SOE saboteurs in the South of France - Tony Brooks DSO, MC. One hopes and prays that the examples of men like Albert and Tony will live on.

It is August and a heatwave and the cricket season has a month still to go. Yet I must adjust my thoughts. I am standing on Rye Golf Course and observing the constant passage of members whose minds are only on their afternoon's round of golf. It is four weeks since rain last fell in the Marsh and conditions are a little unusual. Standing near the old Golf Links Station, almost everything is brown between myself and the clubhouse, and the fairways seem to be almost white. A few hawthorn, buckthorn and gorse bushes break the colour sequence, together with the greens. The golfers themselves offer further contrast in colour, with their blue, white or green uppers. They offer a lesson, too, in dedication and determination; the mid-afternoon heat is intense.

I venture further onto the course and immediately six partridges take off almost at my feet. They are well camouflaged in the rough grass, unusually brown and dry, as are most of the wild flowers. Coltsfoot and ragwort are the exception and still retaining some flower and colour. Even the thistles have gone to seed and are dying rapidly. Two common blues flit gently among the grasses. A few yards on and a skylark flies up into the hawthorn ahead of me and I fix it in my binoculars to savour the sighting a little longer. Larks remain moderately common in Romney Marsh but no longer in the Weald generally.

A slight breath of sea air reaches me and I retrace my steps at once across the old railway to the river and gaze down upon the scene. It is low tide and there is plenty of mud. Gulls are circling overhead with their usual strident cries. Here and there they probe the mud and then, frustrated, slip into the water. Low tide or not, the channel is wide enough for a shallow-draught vessel, but all the boats within sight are securely tied up on the mud - large cabin-cruisers, small cabin-cruisers, fishing boats, sailing dinghies, most with names. What lies behind them? Nearest to me are "Freewheeler", "Sandpiper", "Aries" (was the owner an astrologer or just born in that March-April period?) and finally "Rother III", proudly displaying on its cabin roof the words "Harbour Master". It looked a little more ready for immediate use than the others.

Beneath the Harbour Master's Office flew, rather surprisingly, the Belgian flag, various anchors lent visual atmosphere and a crashed Dornier's propeller reminded one that it was a far more likely scene 50 years ago. Motor Torpedo Boats were based there and the railway supplied them. Perhaps one of them even shot down that Dornier on their return from a fruitless night waiting off the enemy coast. Their spirits would have risen and they would have entered the river mouth more proudly, with their White Ensigns flying from the masthead.

Two concerts in three days suggest a music critic or an addict. I do not think I am either. Both concerts were, however, in outstanding village churches, Ivychurch in Romney Marsh and Peasmarsh, East Sussex; the former a cathedral, the latter small by comparison. Contrasts were also very evident in the music - in St. George's, the City of Canterbury Brass Band, which must have reverberated all over Ivychurch itself; in St. Peter & St. Paul, the strings of the Kingsmead Quartet offering the delicate minuets of Haydn.

In St. George's, having positioned myself near a gas fire, I allowed myself to lapse a little into history (both near and far). That grand 14th century building would have experienced an infinite variety of music and liturgy, beginning with the plainsong and prayers of the monks of the monastery, faithfully keeping their daily offices. Later, it would have heard Anglican chants and, in the 1960s, a string quartet accompanying organ and congregation at candle-lit Evensong. And now brass, with tubas and trombones up against the tower screen, dated 1686; on one wing, stood the font where our children were baptised and, near to it, a framed photo of the Archbishop in full regalia, looking on, I feel sure, approvingly. Overhead, where bats often reside, hung two oval text-boards, reminding us all of St. Paul's stern teaching - "Be not deceived: Evil company doth corrupt good manners" and "Let us consider one another to provoke unto love and to good works". Having held ourselves back from joining in with "Men of Harlech" and the "Lincolnshire Poacher", we finished with a March which was undoubtedly Light Infantry and left us breathless.

St. Peter & St. Paul, Peasmarsh, offered a contrast. Instead of wide open spaces, it stood in a park-like setting. Other things were rather different, including the audience - the music, dare one say, was a little highbrow. Furthermore, it was also a Flower Festival and, immediately, in the porch, one paused. On the seat was a yellow and green arrangement captioned "Hare and Hounds"! Did this mean that the theme was country sports or Sussex pubs or animals? Discreet enquiry revealed that none were right. There was (regrettably) no theme but some financial backing. The skill of floral art was evident on all sides but memorable was the Primary School effort of strongly coloured bowls against a "reredos" of paper giraffes and elephants and, secondly, a magnificent waterfall creation with rocks, moss and wild flowers - an engineering feat as well.

Soon we settled down to listen with much enjoyment to four highly professional musicians offering us two Haydn quartets and another by Borodin. Moreover, the printed programme gave us the luxury of a short score of the themes of each movement. So we easily slipped back into the 18th century era of great composers. The evening concluded with some "box and cox" manoeuvring and an excellent supper in the west end of the church. We were each allowed half a bottle of wine and I thought how appropriate it was that my table was immediately under the six (new) bell-ropes. Bellringers have always had the reputation of good drinkers.

August for me has always meant Canterbury Cricket Week. These days, because of overcrowded fixture lists, the Week is reduced to a Festival Match. Nevertheless, it still retains the air of the oldest Cricket Week in the country. The marquees, the hats on Ladies Day and the military band combine to suggest that history and tradition can still be part of the modern cricket scene. Moreover, town and country come together each year on that lovely St. Lawrence Ground. Village cricketers and senior members of the Band of Brothers and longstanding Kent supporters from Dartford all rub shoulders round the ground and all have definite opinions as to why the Kent opening batsmen failed that morning.

Ladies Day this year ran true to form. Kent were batting on the second day and, even before play began, the ground was rapidly filling up and well-dressed ladies, with hats prominent, were already parading round the marquees and stands. Moreover, in due course, the Kent batsmen went on to score freely and happily, finally to pass the 500 mark, the highest total at Canterbury since 1923. Several 6s went deep into the stands and twice the ball was lost for several minutes and then found by small boys, exuberant with pride.

Lunch for your scribe was with old friends from Hythe Cricket Club, quite informal and relaxed in the open air. Its location was a little unusual - within the structure and shadow of the great sightscreen at the Nackington road end. It was risky. One just hoped that it would not need to be moved, because of some bowler deciding to bowl round the wicket. Conversation and security would have ceased abruptly. Conversation did, in fact, pause over coffee when Corinne, a French friend, swept into our circle, all elegance and fashion and coquetry. She held all eyes. She seemed almost to have stepped out of the Arabian Nights - a cream and gold waistcoat over a claret blouse, with long flowing trousers, and silver and gold bangles round waist and wrist, the whole, crowned with a wide-brimmed straw hat and two beautiful roses. For a while it was difficult to remember the cricket.

Back for the afternoon's viewing from the pavilion annexe, I was pleased to see just above me in the roof a pair of feral pigeons. There were indulging in their usual courtship display and doing some nest repairs for yet another brood. In the 1950s, swallows always nested there and regularly swept across the pitch, almost within arm's length of the fieldsmen. I think that I did read that one day cover-point caught one, thinking it was the ball.

A brief holiday on the edge of the Cotswolds brought me new colours as well as change of scenery. The village of Marshfield, standing on the ridge, offers long views and rows of period stone-built houses and cottages, huddled tidily round the parish church and ancient market-place. The latter contained the usual medley of pick-ups and cars but, more conspicuously, an Alvis Scout Car of the 1950s, camouflaged and Union Jacks painted fore and aft. Like an old horse, it was enjoying a peaceful end to its life in the hands of a military enthusiast. Round the corner was the Lord Nelson Inn which could, I suppose, claim the privilege of flying the White Ensign; in spite of its offer of good food, it gave the impression of being a typical seamen's pub found in ports the world over in pre-War years.

The main street was a joy compared with, shall we say, Rolvenden High Street. There was no through traffic; shoppers could park and talk without the intrusion of noise or rush. Even the shops were aesthetically in tune with the houses - no gaudy frontages, but a steady stream of customers who clearly responded to quality inside. One front, larger than some, caught my eye; on either side of the proprietor's name over the door, were the two words "Pet" and "Garden". Inside, I stepped back 100 years; not only was the building "listed" but the Edwardian and Victorian fittings were as well - two long counters and, behind them, a network of cubby-holes, containing anything from tins of dog-food to fertilizer. The whole shop had that old-fashioned smell that suggests a mixture of candles, cheese, bacon and biscuit. Moreover, the proprietor called me "sir" and was ready to serve me. On my way back up the street, I sampled the Catherine Wheel, a pub of some distinction. The main door, flanked by colourful, overflowing window-boxes, had, over it, a lovely white "shell hood", typical of the West Country. Inside, there were high Victorian chairs at the bar, an armchair or two and windows in keeping with the Georgian style.

The highlight of the day for me was still to come - Choral Evensong in Edington Priory, led by two professional choirs; in the nave, boys and lay clerks drawn from seven cathedrals and, in the chancel, the Consort Singers. No wonder that the BBC were broadcasting it on Radio 3; it was church music at its best. Nothing uplifted me more than when the nave choir sang Psalm 104 to a glorious Anglican chant by Aldrich - "O Lord, how manifold are thy works; in wisdom hast thou made them all; the earth is full of thy riches".

O ur village churches are a treasure. By their very presence in a community, they speak of God. They are also reservoirs of hidden history. Last Sunday I celebrated early Communion in the imposing screened chancel of Etchingham Parish Church. The monks from Robertsbridge probably said their daily offices there, 500 years ago, in those same stalls with their carved misericords. On the altar, lit by eight candles, I read from an altar book in use since Queen Victoria's day. No efficient Rector had crossed out her name or imposed another upon it. I felt, a

shade more than usual, part of history and the timeless message of the Christian Church. How many priests, I wondered, had read from that altar book? I sensed also the merging of scholarship and craftsmanship in that book and its 14th century setting that Christianity has always inspired down the centuries.

However, a little later in the morning, I was brought right up to date. I was leading a Family Communion, slanted towards the children and, in my hand, a 1996 booklet, copiously illustrated, annotated and an abbreviated Rite A Service. Hot air balloons, Arabs in fast cars, people in hospital, ducks, dogs and doves, all those and more, festooned the pages. Just a glimpse of life today, and all needing to be offered to Almighty God.

The previous day, if I maybe forgiven a slight pun, I had been brought right down to earth by the Autumn Flower Show. Sadly, entries were down, and especially the flower classes, so lovely autumnal colours were not too evident. Only a few dahlias and four Michaelmas Daisy entries. I suppose that we gardeners must plan and plant for a change in weather pattern and mulch more intensively. The Autumn is often linked, of course, with earwigs and craneflies - the former mate in the Autumn and the latter hatch out. Both seem to be very active in my house. Daddy-longlegs can be distressingly suicidal, too, whether it is in a cup of coffee or the bath water.

Pride rather than nostalgia dictates this week's subject-matter. June 4th saw the last ships leave the burning port of Dunkirk and June 6th saw the greatest invasion armada ever arrive back on the coast of France. Only two days separate those momentous dates and how appropriate - I believe that the latter would not have been possible without the former. 340,000 Allied troops were rescued by the "little ships" between May 27th and June 4th 1940 in Operation Dynamo. Two weeks ago I gazed upon the small open fishing-boat, the "Tamzine" from Margate in the Imperial War Museum and I marvelled. One week ago I was in the Ellen Terry Barn Theatre and listened to Gary Montgomery impersonating his uncle and at once I was re-living those momentous days.

We were under canvas in the wood adjoining Southwick House, Portsmouth, the Invasion HQ, and a small cog in a vast operation. We had known for weeks the landing area in Normandy, a frightening responsibility. Never to be forgotten was that night of June 5th, standing on the lawns of Southwick House, looking up at the airborne forces overhead and the RAF bombers on their separate missions to blunt the coastal defences. My diary records for June 6th:-

"Invasion has begun... weather just good enough for landing...services held in churches all over England...3 British Div. landed with few casualties and beaches definitely held...Press conference in village hall at 3 pm and at 4 pm they were addressed by Monty..."

For us who served with him, Monty was synonymous with "victory". He instilled this belief in us all. We trusted him, not least because we knew that he cared about people; no lives would be wasted in hasty operations. On that momentous day of June 6th, we who stood on the shore saluted the immense courage of the assault force. For some it was the longest day; for others, sadly, it was their shortest. We all knew, however, that it had to be done; we were fighting for the basic freedoms of speech, worship and democratic way of life, as well as the particular things like family life, cricket on the green and our lovely countryside. One or two of us slipped into the medieval village church and simply prayed.

Nevertheless, that great invasion had originated, I suspect, in the miracle of Dunkirk four years earlier. But for those "little ships" from rivers, estuaries and harbours, the majority of those 340,000 would have been prisoner and no longer a threat to invasion. It was a miracle, I believe, in a deeper, more Biblical sense. Against all the predictions and normal weather behaviour, the seas stayed calm for those ten days. The Almighty had intervened in the natural working of His world. Evil was about to triumph over good. So I finish with the silhouette of one of the "little ships", the Lady Isabelle, belonging to a friend of mine. She was requisitioned from Tims' yard at Staines and is shown exactly as she sailed across the Channel, with a small machine-gun mounted in her bows, prepared to defend herself against Hitler's dive-bombers to the last.

Early in October, in the midst of St. Luke's "little summer", I was privileged to share in a lovely country wedding in Hertfordshire. The bride came from the Old Vicarage, so had no need of Rolls-Royces or carriage and pair, only having to stroll across the intervening parsonage field on the arm of her father to the church. Close by was the marquee and a quartet tuning up and preparing themselves for the eventual return of the guests. In due course we did return and were immediately introduced to the champagne and, later, a marvellous meal in the peach-lined marquee. But this, of course, is not the whole story. Receptions are lengthy affairs these days and certain facilities are essential for the guests. These facilities were manifestly and easily available in the gracious Victorian Old Vicarage nearby — comfortable armchairs, of course, an Aga for heating baby's milk and, above all, a downstairs cloakroom which was the most exciting and the most comfortable that I have ever come across. It deserved detailed consideration.

As a start, it was a real room, measuring 15 feet by 9. As you entered, you were immediately aware of the subdued roar of the boiler, strategically placed to give continuous comfort to all users of the loo itself. Beside them on the other side, they had the company of three bulging golf bags and an umbrella stand, even more bulging, containing lacrosse, hockey and shooting sticks, tennis racquets, one cricket bat but no umbrella. Whatever the sporting talent, there was ample stimulus for endless silent

reminiscences of games won, or only just lost and, one hopes, of worthy opponents. If, however, the user of the loo was non-sporting but historically or socially minded they could enjoy on the opposite wall a great array of family photos stretching back 100 years - grandpa as a boy on the beach with bucket and whip, grandma as a 17 year old, riding side-saddle on her favourite horse, babies, baptisms, weddings and all sorts of school teams. Utterly fascinating and rivetting, even to the casual visitor. As a contrast, in the opposite far corner, were two framed and dignified team photos of the bride's paternal grandfather, international footballer and Kent County cricketer, in his Cambridge University days in the 1920s, youthful, determined and confident of meeting any soccer or cricket side in the country.

There is more to come. Quite properly, near the door, were the conventional medley of coats, mackintoshes and anoraks, seemingly underpinned by rows of wellies. One wondered if occasionally there was not some interchange between them and the contents of the stout travelling trunk under the window, which once belonged to great grandmother and was now the family dressing-up box. Opening its lid, you were at once greeted by a splendid ostrich boa, once favoured by Victorian ladies. Moving to the door, with some reluctance, I found a rocking-horse without any rockers and learned that it had been rescued from a rubbish dump four miles away and repainted before taking an honoured place in this marvellous collection of memorabilia. At that moment the horse had rather a drunken appearance, as the previous user of the nearby wash-basin had tossed the towel haphazardly over its head; I could not help but re-fold it and reverently place it on the saddle. In a last lingering glance I realised that, beside the loo, a Victoria & Albert Christmas catalogue was inviting the user to plan her Christmas shopping at the same time. How could one possibly emerge from that fascinating cloakroom in under half an hour?

Hythe, though not a village, has an attractive rural cricket ground. It has always been the favourite in my playing career and last week I paid it a visit, my first for several years. It was also the very first day that the club (once my club) could legally say that it owned the ground, a proud moment for both negotiators and money-raisers.

So Oliver and I walked slowly and proudly round the long boundary. The main features were just as always and rather rural - the Royal Military Canal and the sea bordering it north and south respectively, tennis courts and allotments on the east and the tree-lined Ladies Walk on the west, once the promenade for crinolined ladies walking from town to seafront. No houses closeby but space and sky and sea-breezes.

As we walked, memories of faithful spectators round the boundary easily returned. There was Emily, who knew most of our names and often took the collecting-box round and was a little feared, being vocally critical if we failed her out in the middle. Further round sat old Dick on a rough bench, his face tanned and capped, leaning on a gnarled stick and his fluffy-tailed mongrel stretched out near him - until provoked into circling antics by my Jack Russell. Into the pavilion enclosure came other regulars, usually vice-presidents. Among them, old Colonel Adams, who watched the cricket silently and intently as if watching inter-regimental polo in India when the honour of the regiment was at stake. Close, but not too close, sat the Reverent Chastel de Boinville (nicknamed at College "Just on the boil, Bill") who called in after encouraging the tennis players. Ex-Vicar of Hythe, old "de B" was excellent company and loved by all in his most active retirement. Inside the pavilion, quietly watching through the same open window, sat Ray Munds, groundsman, ex-Kent 2nd X1 and the steadiest umpire I have ever played under. If he raised his finger, we knew we were out; we trusted him implicitly and, if asked, he invariably gave us supremely wise advice about our performance in the middle. Real gold.

Rising up behind the pavilion lay the town, like some silent amphitheatre crowd and dominated by the great parish church of St. Leonard's, with its Norman nave and, in John Newman's words, "the grandest chancel of any non-monastic church in the County". Moreover, to seal the connection between Church and cricket, we usually had the Vicar and his curate both playing. Besides being our chairman, "Bobs" Newman, the Vicar, was a leading statistician and could easily tell you how many centuries Leslie Ames had made in his career or how old Douglas Wright was. John, the curate, was in a slightly different category. We often wondered if there was a special clause in his contract which obliged him to play for the club and serve behind the bar afterwards. Be that as it may, John was a good cricketer but seldom attained his true form in the field or with the bat. We excused him on the grounds that he was groping for a text for tomorrow's sermon, which could have been a verse from St. Paul's second letter to Timothy -

"And if also a man contend in the games, he is not crowned except he have contended lawfully".

In the country it is the time of year for Annual General Meetings. I should have been at three this past week. As it was, I cried off one, that of the local cricket club, because Brock was so sick and miserable that I could not possibly leave him alone. Now, AGMs are often a real test of Chairmanship, partly because their structure is slanted towards participation by "the floor" and, in particular, through that open-ended last item "AOB". There is the further crucial matter of the meeting's venue. The Royal British Legion's AGM was in a pub and the Gardening Society's in the Village Hall. There are advantages and disadvantages in a pub. On the one hand, there is a convivial atmosphere and refreshment easily available; on the other hand, there is usually background music and more argument, stimulated by the refreshment. I still have clear memories of 'chairing' my local cricket club's AGM in a pub some years ago.

Theoretically we met in a room, but it was a room in name only. It had three doors. One led directly into the bar and counter, the second, into the ladies' cloakroom and the third, into a rear entrance to the kitchens. It needs little imagination to realise that progress was painfully slow. After three years, I said "no more".

One would have thought that the Village Hall was a safe venue for our Gardening Society, but there are hazards there. We had hardly got past "Apologies for absence" and "Minutes of the 1997 AGM" when many of us realised that we could not hear. The overhead gas heater gave us warmth but neutralised audibility. We chose the latter and listened to the President's Address, but within a few minutes of the start of the Chairman's Report the nearby church bells opened up and continued for the next hour. The front two rows understandably led the comment and discussion but all had views on the proposed relaxation of Show Rules. They felt that it would not lead to more exhibits, even if marrows, courgettes and dahlias were allowed to be smaller. Most gardeners naturally compare and challenge other people's produce. In any case, the lowest common denominator is a poor stimulant and, as one member said, the answer may be simply "more manure". The remaining items, even membership subscription, were rapidly disposed of, in the manner of a waiter clearing away empty glasses on the morning after. AOB was greeted with a loud plea for "a glass of wine". All the meeting the bottles had been standing invitingly behind the Chairman.

M y friend, Rachel, is moving away to another County after 21 years in a lovely family house. I and many others are very sad indeed. But, on the other hand, those 21 years have been wonderfully active and happy and fruitful for the local parish church and the community. An example, perhaps, to others who are endowed with the good things of this life, but may not recognise their stewardship.

"Trowswell" may have begun life as a nunnery in Elizabethan days. As possible evidence, the roof supports a tiny bell-turret to call the residents to prayer and, deep in the interior of the house, can be found a priest's hole, a reminder of religious persecution. Later generations have added further rooms and refinements for it to become, to the uncritical eye, a large late Victorian house, complete with conservatory, greenhouses, mellow garden walls, paddocks and fine trees. A veritable paradise for all ages, especially children and dogs.

Such a paradise existed during Rachel and Jim's tenure. Gardens and animals were an utterly natural part of their consciousness and personalities. Whether family or visitor, one was immediately sucked into the rhythm of rural activity - it might be feeding chickens and bantams or picking grapes in the greenhouses or walking Rachel's beloved Norfolk terriers round the paddocks. This latter exercise was often made quite exciting by the donkeys (Rachel's other love) who invariably charged strange dogs, including Brock. And yet it seemed almost 'infra dig' to run, because, towering above us, was the central feature of both house and garden - a grand avenue of mighty Wellingtonias. Dignity and longevity, combined. Beneath them, I usually felt small and temporary. They dominated everything and everyone.

But, of course, Rachel and Jim belonged to church and community and always had lots of time for both. Out of "Trowswell" came warm friendship, frequent hospitality and regular worship of Almighty God "from whom all good things do come". Dear Rachel, small of stature but big of heart, we all "wish you good luck, in the name of the Lord".

Last week-end I watched with quiet delight my first cricket match of the season. It was a village contest, as it should be, between Rolvenden and Hurst Green, a sort of pre-view of Kent v Sussex at Hove. The weather was fair to middling; the sun came and went and a few sweaters were worn - not too bad for the last day of April. By the time of my arrival the Rolvenden opening bowlers had spent their force and first change were on - slowish off-breaks from one end and medium outswingers from the other. Runs came steadily, if slowly, occasionally with the help of the traditional cross-bat. Even more occasionally, wickets fell, one a run-out as the result of a scorching return from third man. Full marks to fieldsman and wicketkeeper, so early in the season. Spectators were not exactly numerous - two on a bench, one in a deckchair among the players and a West Highland terrier keeping its master company on the grassy boundary. But, of course, all this time the ladies were preparing tea in the pavilion, an essential part of any cricket match. So the visitors declared at tea with 153 on the board, with off-breaker, Jason, claiming four wickets. It was indeed the day for slow bowlers. Rolvenden, with one exception, were demolished by Hurst Green's leg-break bowler for the modest total of 87. Other captains, please note! Leg-breakers (of which your scribe was one) do sometimes deliver the goods.

Watching that match stirred deeper thoughts of 50 years ago. Victory in Europe had restored once more for me the vision of cricket on the village greens of Kent. It came a close third to home and family and career as among the most valued things that we were fighting for and might, please God, one day return to. I suspect that many other Men of Kent and Kentish Men felt the same. Over those War years, some of us may have had some very occasional cricket - of a sort. There was some mixed cricket at Southwick House, Portsmouth, with a red-headed Wren as wicketkeeper. There was a matting-on-concrete wicket in an orchard at Iserlohn, Westphalia and, above all, there was an immaculate grass wicket in the middle of a concrete cycle track at Dortmund, undamaged amid the utter devastation, not a building standing for miles. It kept hope alive and reminded the ear of the sound of bat on ball, but all those moments were a mere shadow of the real thing. This came at last during that long hot summer of 1947, cricket ad infinitum from May to September.

The churchyard at Lympne, once visited, is not easily forgotten. Its commanding position on the ridge gives you miles of view the length of Romney Marsh. One can stand at the end for a full hour and still recognise more objects and more landmarks. Being a winter's day and moderately clear, we could distinguish Dungeness lighthouse and the twin power stations beyond it on that distant curve of the bay. In the middle and near distances there grazed hundreds of sheep among the criss-cross pattern of the dykes, full to overflowing from recent rains and stretching away to the sea margin.

The churchyard may have this commanding position, but, even more exciting, it sits astride 1700 years of history. Below us, on the grassy slopes, were the solid remains of the third century Roman fort, guarding the port serving that great sea bay, now rich pasture and thriving communities. A few yards behind us stood the massive Norman tower of St. Stephen's Church, and almost touching, as if in solidarity, the mass of Lympne Castle, in origin a medieval manor house, later an Archdeacon's palace and a farmhouse, and, more recently, a gentleman's residence. In the 1939-45 War it almost became a real castle; Royal Engineers and Newfoundland Artillery occupied it and left their contribution to its architecture in the glass-fronted observation post at the very top of its low tower. What treasure for the historian on that one spot!

But we were gathered there to pay our last respects to Clara and to give thanks for a truly good person. She epitomized the rural character. Steady, reliable, content, slow of speech, she had been a very active part of church and community life for the last 55 years. With husband, Robert, away on Active Service with the anti-aircraft guns defending the Kent coast, Clara "dug for victory" in the local market garden and then helped Robert run the village shop as well as play the church organ on Sundays for 50 years. In spite of her quiet presence, everyone knew her and everyone loved her. We could not remember a critical word coming from her. So we laid her to rest with Robert in a corner of this historic churchyard, not far from the so-called "Airmen's Corner". On these War Graves Commission headstones were some familiar names, among them "Reginald Dupe, Sgt Pilot, RAF, killed in action in the Battle of Britain" and "Bill Davis, Chief Instructor Cinque Ports Flying Club", also "An Unknown Airman of the 1939-45 War, but known unto God", all reminders of Lympne aerodrome's part in peace and war. The church bells in that Norman tower should have rung out that day for Clara and those airmen, fiercely proclaiming their message of joy and freedom and Christian love right across the Marsh to Dymchurch Redoubt and the sea.

A view causes most people to pause or stop. Such is the effect upon me of the breathtaking view from above Catt Farm, Stone in Oxney. Facing east, with the ground falling away rapidly, one has the immediate impression of miles of lush cultivated countryside. Fields and trees predominate. There seems to be scarcely a building. Chapel Bank stands out in the middle distance; before it, patches of oil-seed rape and, on all sides, acres of young two foot high corn, with occasional wooded areas. And then, as one concentrates, Woodchurch windmill is visible and, on the far left, Barrack Farm and, on the right, Court Lodge, Appledore and its parish church of St. Peter & St. Paul. Below it, the Royal Military Canal and shades of Napoleon and threatened invasion.

As I stood there, I remembered another threatened invasion in May 1940 and Anthony Eden broadcasting for volunteers to meet it. "Join the Local Defence Volunteers and defend your village and your home". Within hours the LDV (later the Home Guard) was born. My viewpoint was the ideal observation post for the Home Guard. Indeed, beside me was a derelict building with a sapling growing out of it, which might conceivably have begun life as a shelter during those tense summer nights of 1940 but much more recently may have been a collection point for hundreds of strawberries grown in that field. They were days that all of us who were involved will always remember. As Anthony Armstrong wrote in his book "Village at War" -

> "Those June and July nights up the hill were very beautiful.
> Dusk was generally setting in about the time the first patrol
> arrived and the calm sweeps of turf billowed away to either
> side. Below, the Wealden countryside...was laid out like a
> map and treated like a map, too; all were landmarks and we
> knew the distances and direction of them for reporting
> parachutists..."

My view certainly had two distant structural landmarks - Woodchurch windmill and Tenterden parish church tower. Though some six miles away, a signal lamp on either would have been visible and readable to the Home Guards above Catt Farm. One imagines them in that fine summer of 1940 regularly on night watch from that vantage point or from the pill-box on the ridge overlooking the vast open spaces of Romney Marsh. The remainder of the patrol would probably have been more happily stationed below at the Ferry Inn, guarding the bridge over the dyke and standing by the telephone in the public bar!

Your scribe has just spent a week in Pembury Hospital. Entry to hospital can be a shock to anyone but I suspect that it can be more so to the countryman. From my bed in a large ward on the upper floor of the main block, my "view" was simply of more roof, one feral pigeon and blue sky. The usual daily sights surrounding a house in the country were missing - no snowdrops, no blackbird catching the early worm, no squirrel doing a mischief to the nut container.

Then, unexpectedly, came a large bowl of mixed Spring plants from generous

friends. I had a miniature garden right beside me on my table! Wonderful! A clump of narcissus, a large white hyacinth, a multiflowering yellow pansy, a cluster of tiny red flowers, all surrounded by variegated and spidery greenery. Morale took a further uplift from my first three "Get Well" cards. A large barn owl helped my thoughts drift back to local barns and this ghostly bird "quartering" the fields near me. A king-fisher, inevitably perched on a sign "No Fishing", reminded me of the last ecstatic sighting on the Rother near Newenden bridge. My third gave me the contrast of Jacob sheep and lambs at Penshurst, being fed under a spreading oak in typical parkland. All was now well. I had countryside round my bed and, as a bonus, a senior much respect-ed fly-fisherman in the next bed; he always wore his fly-fishing tie but was so short of breath that conversation was limited.

But, of course, I was there to get better from my pneumonia condition and I could not have been in a better place. In this acutely-ill medical ward there always seemed bustle and activity. Doctors, and nurses especially, seldom stopped. Tolerance, cheerfulness, energy and lighthearted-chat went alongside medical caring. It was truly uplifting. At the end of the day, the last hot drink and the drug round led impercep-tively into quiet and dimmed lights. Some poor souls could not sleep or breathe but, at the touch of a button, a nurse would come. Inevitably, the ghost of Florence Nightingale and her lamp came to mind; at night, especially, her spirit lives on. To me the nights were never lonely, always being assured of the ready support of night staff, willing even just to talk, if sleep would not come.

My recovery was greatly assisted by one other factor - the food. I could hardly believe how good it was. A choice of three dishes for each course resulted the next day in a personal container, and in it each course, delicious and attractively presented. Caterer and chef deserve Egon Ronay status.

My last day, Sunday, I was moved into a "Going home" ward. One of the nurses there (male and Falstaffian figure) enjoyed singing as he did his rounds. His favourite seemed to be "Oh, I do like to be beside the seaside..." but being Sunday he once lapsed into a hymn "Who would true valour see, Let him come hither...". Valour was needed and present in that hospital from many patients and doctors and nurses.

PROFILES

MR. JIM HOAD

Jim might be described as the most successful Rolvenden boy of the post-war generation. With an education entirely confined to the Primary School, he in due course founded and directed a flourishing sausage-making firm with national outlets and also became Mayor of Ashford Borough Council, mixing with the highest in the land.

Arriving in the village at the age of four, Jim sometimes helped his father deliver the bread he had baked in Rolvenden Layne, before leaving school at 14 and joining Woodgate, builders, at High Halden, to be followed a few years later with an apprenticeship with Sainsbury's Meat Department at Ashford. So began his long career in the butchery and meat industry.

Having met and married Janet, Jim launched his own shop in the High Street in 1959 and developed a busy trade until the supermarkets began to alter shopping habits. Undeterred, he specialised in sausages, set up his village factory and produced Hoad's Korkers, with great success and flair. Soon afterwards, in 1984, he was elected to represent Rolvenden and the Layne and Newenden on the Borough Council and has continued to do so ever since, in his last two elections receiving the highest majority and number of votes of any councillor. In 1994-5 he was asked to be Mayor and, typically, put all his energy, enthusiasm and talents into that year of office. His memories of that period include attendance in St. Paul's Cathedral of the VE Day Anniversary Thanksgiving, in Chelsea Hospital for the 6th Airborne Division's 50th Anniversary celebrations and a goodwill visit to Virginia, USA, on behalf of Ashford Council. A further distinction was to be with Keith Speed MP in the first small group to use the Channel Tunnel.

All these years the village has been his base and inspiration. Earlier the Cricket Club benefited from his playing; his fast medium bowling brought him a remarkable 297 wickets in one season and his lbw appeals would wake up any umpire. Newenden Cricket Club record Jim as having scored 117 in 41 minutes against the Mount at Crawley. If pressed, Jim points to his fortunate legacy of the wartime spirit that pervaded the whole country, to enterprise and quite a lot of luck, and to consistent hard work. Always behind these years of effort and service have been his family life and his children, his gardens and the trees and ponds in them and the wild life. All these and other strands have anchored Jim most happily to his own village of Rolvenden.

MR. GORDON STONHAM

Gordon has been at the centre of Rolvenden life for over 40 years. Moreover, those years have revolved entirely round farming and the community, embracing both work and leisure.

The seeds were sown before the War in another Kent village, Chartham, near Canterbury. Here Gordon grew up on a farm and, except for a few years of War service, he has spent his life farming. His War service in the Indian Army introduced him to other climates and crops and vegetation, not just in India but also Malaya and Java, where the Japanese were being slow to surrender. Peacetime allowed him time for study at Nottingham University and a year's practical experience at Sissinghurst Castle Farm under Captain Beale, succeeded by three years on a livestock farm in Lincolnshire and marriage to Sheila. All this, a sound preparation for his manager's job at Hole Park Farms in 1955 and his life's work.

The original two farms grew in number as tenants gave up and his responsibilities increased to include hops, fruit, dairy, sheep and vegetables and, at one time, 22 regular employees. In those early years those farms represented the mainstream of village life. They were important financially as well as visually. Among Gordon's earliest memories of the village were Mr. Savill, the Vicar, driving around in his smart Singer car and the prompt visit of the organist who soon had Gordon in the choir, in which he still sings; this inevitably led to many years on the PCC and sterling work, with Ken Elliott and Leslie Codgbrook, running the village Youth Club. The list of voluntary community activities is almost endless - Weald of Kent Round Table, Tenterden Lions, Rother Valley Farmers and, above all, the Weald of Kent Ploughing Match. Gordon was specially proud of this event, which included the only hop-drying competition, except the brewers'; committee member and Chairman, he finished up as President.

Through all these years and all these activities was a quietly-spoken, philosophical, tolerant man, a very good friend to many in the village. Such he remains in retirement, still giving of his best to local life, but spending more time in his garage. In it resides his beloved Morris 8 two-seater tourer and, beside it, the chassis and body of yet another Morris 8 tourer!

MRS MARJORIE MONK

Marjorie has contributed to Rolvenden village life for the remarkable period of about 50 years. Leaving aside sport, it is difficult to find any society or activity in which she has not participated at one time or another. Moreover, she is still involved at an age when most people have already handed over to others younger.

Born and bred in Ashford, Marjorie left school at 14 and went into service as kitchen maid in my own home village of Lympne and with a family whom I knew well.

Unknowingly, we must have met. Over four happy years she learned a lot about cooking, which was to enable her to become cook to old Mrs. Woodd at Kingsgate shortly before the War. So began a very long and faithful period of service with the Woodd family which continued till Mrs. Diana Woodd's death a few years ago. In the meantime other important things had happened. She met and married a Rolvenden Layne man in 1940 and gave birth to their first born in 1941. She also joined the Maytham Hall staff as a part-time assistant and remained as such for 25 years.

Amazingly, Marjorie still had time for other things, which always included active communicant membership of the parish church. Over those post war years she has been a standard-bearer for the Royal British Legion and a long-serving poppy-seller, the Primary School caretaker, a member of the Maytham Players and a leading light of the Over 60s. Her energy is still amazing. It is seldom that anything takes place in the Village Hall but that Marjorie is not involved and usually through the "hatchway", offering refreshments and cakes with her typical welcoming smile. Somehow, it seems absolutely right that she now sings in the church choir. It is expressive of an attitude to life. This has meant serving cheerfully her own family, the Woodd family, her friends and her village - "O praise ye The Lord"

A PERSONAL TRIBUTE TO MARY BEAUMONT

Mary Beaumont could have stepped straight out of one of Trollope's novels. She typified many a country rector's wife of the late Victorian era. Tall, angular, crisp in speech and often in tweeds, Mary saw her role and her duty as one who should know and care for all her husband's parishioners as well as give an example in matters of Faith and churchgoing. Her interests anyway were those of country people - horses, riding, dogs, gardening and wildlife. Her Christian Faith was of her childhood and definite and founded four-square on the Church of England, its sacraments and its Book of Common Prayer. She had little time for doubters and, in a wider context, for ditherers and psychoanalysts. Her comment was invariably forthright but her style, courteous. Not surprisingly, Mary was proud of her country and World War II saw both herself and her husband, Godfrey, in Army uniform. Eventually retirement from the parish of Teston, near Maidstone, brought them to their Rolvenden cottage, surrounded by woods and farmland and cock pheasants calling. All of this was a delight to Mary's eye and ear and, after Godfrey's death, she was quietly content with her daily routine of gardening and dog walks. Sunday mornings, of course, brought her to the parish church and in the front pew, providing that her ancient car had started up. From that pew she led the congregational prayers and concluded the others with a loud "Amen". Like many real "characters", Mary was wonderfully stimulating and surprisingly lovable. Moveover she stood for attitudes and a way of life that have made this country great in the past and may, please God, one day be recovered.

MEMORIAL SERVICE - PATIENCE STRONG

How appropriate in a way - St. Nicholas Day and the memorial service for one of our very own congregation in St. Bride's Fleet Street! Angela and I felt proud of Winifred and were proud to represent St. Nicholas, Sandhurst at this service. This was our first glimpse of St. Bride's, the printers' church, re-built, restored and re-dedicated in 1957 in the presence of Her Majesty the Queen. Outside, office workers and a few printers scurrying around in their lunch-hour break, three No. 9 buses in a row and Hulton's Weekly still proclaiming the tradition of the Street. Inside, a typical restored City church. Art, craftsmanship and theology unified to create a lovely place of worship of the God of all Creation. A churchwarden, dignified and gowned, greeted us and placed us, happily, beside the choir, who were young and professional and, I venture to say, the best part of the service. They uplifted us all with their Introit (my favourite motet) Redford's "Rejoice in the Lord alway", echoing surely the tone of many of Winifred's letters to worried and confused enquirers all through her long, literary life. Bible readings and her own poems and hymn and a lovely anthem "Laudate Dominum" all preceded a very personal tribute by Doreen Montgomery, her agent, stressing her enormous and therapeutic appeal to 'the man in the street' all her life. Lonely house-wives and fearful servicemen were all sustained by her - by letter and poem. Few fan mails can have had such healing property. Thank God for Winifred Cushing and her regular presence in the second row of our Mission Church, for her humility and generosity and her love for all mankind.

MRS. BESSIE ELLIOTT

Bessie Elliott (née Britcher) is one of the most gentle, kindly and courteous people in Rolvenden. She and her husband, Ken, each in their own way, had an unusually wide influence upon the young of the village in 25 or more post-war years. It helped form many a character in those impressionable early years.

Bessie was born in Rolvenden Layne and, except for short periods, has spent all her life, living and working in this village. The Primary School and Ashford County Grammar School eventually led her to Brighton Training College to learn about teaching the 3 Rs and music to infants; Red Cross Auxiliary work at Brighton Hospital occupied some of the holidays as well as helping back home with the hopping, usually at Friezingham where her father was the old-fashioned type of worker who could turn his hand to anything on the farm.

Peace brought marriage to Ken and a bit of shuffling around of jobs, Bessie obtaining a post at Hayes Primary (Ken's home) only to find Ken accepting a Craft Teaching job in Tenterden! In the end all was sorted out and Bessie was appointed to Rolvenden Primary and stayed here for about 30 years, often teaching more than one generation of a family, all to the enormous benefit of the children. As one headmaster said "Bessie was a dedicated teacher and had a great love of children. There was no one better to introduce infants to school life".

That is not, of course, the end of her story. She was Chairman of the local Guides Support Group and found time for the Mother's Union and Young Wives and particularly the Junior Church. Her music led to involvement in the Schools Weald of Kent Music Festival and local pantomimes. She also sang with Tenterden Choral Society and the St. Peter' Singers at Newenden. Some years, she was invited to sing that moving opening verse of "Once in Royal David's City". Then one heard the timbre and quality of a cathedral chorister. A pure voice, in a serene, smiling person.

THE REVEREND RAYMOND HEATH

Raymond Heath, who died rather suddenly in June, will be remembered by many with respect and affection as Vicar of the parish between 1966 and 1975. Like many post-war clergy, Raymond had held a wartime commission. He was in the Royal Warwickshire Regiment and was mentioned in dispatches' twice, in campaigns that included Dunkirk, North Africa and North West Europe. After ordination in Coventry, two curacies (in Radford and Tilehurst) and four years as an Organising Secretary for the Missions to Seamen preceded his first parish appointment as Vicar of Walmer.

So Raymond arrived in Rolvenden with considerable all-round experience and a reputation as a conscientious parish priest with a flair for Family Services in that holiday area. This reputation he enhanced considerably in Rolvenden. His weekly Family Services attracted family and school groups from both inside and outside the parish. Brickwall School, Benenden and Ranters Oak were among the schools. He did not rely (like some modern clergy) on gimmicks and guitars. His style was friendly, simple, down to earth and slightly humorous, without losing the basic dignity of worship. He had a rapport with the young which they enjoyed greatly.

He had a sense of worship generally and all the services in St. Mary's were planned with care and reflected the right balance of dignity and informality. His sermons were invariably crisp and forthright and good.

Round the parish, other things were good - his visiting, his availability for counselling, his organising of meetings and events. Churchwardens and others enjoyed greatly working with him. He and his family were also the first occupants of the new vicarage and his wife, Peggy, had the pleasure of creating a new garden. Early retirement from parish life gave him a locum ministry in the parishes round Stow-on-the-Wold, where he worshipped and sang in the choir. So, after a varied life and most fruitful ministry, Raymond was laid to rest in the churchyard of St. Edward's on June 17th. Thanks be to God.

MISS PENELOPE COX

There can be few more familiar, or more lovable, figures in Rolvenden High Street than Penelope. These days she can often be seen more than once in a morning, having forgotten some important item for her lunch. In addition, there is always conversation with all sorts of people, due simply to her wide involvement with village life over 48 years. Her shopping is not done in five minutes.

Penelope arrived on the Rolvenden scene in 1950, having studied at the Slade School of Art and worked during the War as a draughtswoman in ground radar; as a result, she saw the first V1s to arrive over the coast at the plotting station at Hythe. By the time she arrived in the village she had already been appointed to take charge of the Art Department at Benenden Girls School - entirely as the result of a good letter to the Headmistress. So began her life's work of 25 happy years at the School, teaching among others the Princess Royal. Her work embraced scenery for plays and pageants as well as drawing, painting, bookbinding and calligraphy.

At the same time, Penelope has never forgotten that she is a member of a village community and she has generously given to that community in all sorts of ways. As a basis, she served many years on both the Parish Council and Church Council (12 years as secretary, "when it was a much easier job"). Mary Townsend persuaded her to take over the Christmas Market for a similarly long stint. One suspects, though, that she most enjoyed founding and directing the Flower Festival from 1972 and running the Flower Rota in church. Her artistic talents came fully into action. Worship in St. Mary's has been thereby uplifted over many years and has also had her most regular presence; her calligraphy still beautifies the Baptismal Roll and the In Memoriam panels.

Behind all this activity, in and outside the village, has been an artistic, deeply sensitive person, who has naturally seen God in the world around her, whether in her garden, the countryside or her dogs. She has also seen God in people, hence her long years of service.